Insights from Archaeology

Insights from Archaeology

David A. Fiensy

Fortress Press
Minneapolis

INSIGHTS FROM ARCHAEOLOGY

Cover image: Brooklyn Bridge/Andres Garcia Martin/Thinkstock & Cruz de Tejeda/emregologlu/Thinkstock
Cover design: Alisha Lofgren

Print ISBN: 978-1-5064-0014-3
eBook ISBN: 978-1-5064-0108-9

The paper used in this publication meets the minimum requirements of American National Standard for Information Sciences — Permanence of Paper for Printed Library Materials, ANSI Z329.48-1984.

Manufactured in the U.S.A.

This book was produced using Pressbooks.com, and PDF rendering was done by PrinceXML.

For my siblings: Kitty, Chris, and Deanne
הנה מה טוב ומה נעים שבת אחים גם יחד
(Psalm 133:1)

Contents

Series Foreword

"What does this mean?"

That is, perhaps, the most-asked question with regard to the Bible. What does this verse mean? What does this story mean? What does this psalm or letter or prophecy or promise or commandment mean?

The question can arise from a simple desire for information, or the concern may be one of context or relevance: What *did* this mean to its original audience? What *does* it mean for us today?

Someone has said that understanding the Bible is difficult not because meaning is hard to find but because it is so abundant. The problem for interpreters is not *too little meaning* but *too much*. The question becomes, which of all the possible meanings is to be preferred?

But is that really a problem? And, if so, is it not a lovely one?

This abundance of meaning became especially clear in the last decades of the twentieth century when the field of biblical studies embraced dozens of new methods and approaches that had not previously been used or appreciated within the guild. In many ways, biblical studies became more exciting than ever before.

But, yes, the task of understanding the Bible could be daunting. Bible teachers, clergy and lay, who had struggled through college or seminary to learn "the historical-critical method" were suddenly confronted with novel strategies drawn from many other fields of inquiry: sociology, psychology, world religions, cultural anthropology, communication theory, modern literary criticism, and so forth. Then came the avalanche of interpretive approaches grounded in particular philosophical or ideological perspectives: feminism, postmodernism, liberation theology, postcolonialism, queer theology, and on and on.

For the open minded, the yield was an embarrassment of riches. We now understand the Bible in so many different ways: its historical witness, its theological message, its emotional impact, its sociocultural significance, its literary artistry, its capacity for rhetorical engagement, and so on.

At this point in time, we probably understand the Bible better than any who have gone before us. The Bible may challenge us more deeply than it challenged our forebears—and, yet, we have discovered that the Bible also seems to invite us (perhaps to *dare* us) to challenge it back. Many insights into the meaning of Scripture have come from people doing exactly that.

This *Insights* series from Fortress Press presents brief volumes that describe different ways in which modern scholars approach the Bible, with emphasis on what we have learned from each of these approaches. These are not boring books on esoteric methodology. Some attention, of course, needs to be paid to presumptions and procedures, but the emphasis in each book is on the practical "pay-off" that a given approach has for students and teachers of the Bible. The authors discuss the most important insights they have gained from their approaches and they provide examples of how those insights play out when working with specific biblical texts in actual real-world circumstances.

Each volume discusses:

- how a particular method, approach, or strategy was first developed and how its application has changed over time;

- what current questions arise from its use;

- what enduring insights it has produced; and

- what questions remain for future scholarship.

Some volumes feature traditional approaches while others focus on new and experimental ones. You will definitely learn things in every book. Your current understanding of "what the Bible means" will be increased. And if you find that the "type of meaning" gained from a particular approach is not what interests you, perhaps you will nevertheless be grateful for the brief tour of a topic that fascinates some of your peers. The books are intentionally brief: they allow us to sample strategies and perspectives, to look down various avenues and see where they lead. They facilitate informed decisions regarding where we might want to go next.

I trust that we are now past the point of arguing over which approach to Scripture is the correct one. Such squabbles were part of the growth pains associated with the guild's aforementioned discovery that meaning is abundant, not so much elusive as ubiquitous.

Those of us who were professors during the late twentieth century sometimes helped our students deal with the methodological confusion by reminding them of the old Indian fable about six blind men and an elephant. In one well-known version of that tale, each of the blind men encounters an elephant and decides "what an elephant is like" based on his singular experience: one feels the trunk and says an elephant is like a hose; another, the tusk and says it is like a spear; another, the ear and says it is like a fan; another, the side and says it is like a wall; another, the leg and says it is like a tree; another, the tail and says it is like a rope. Later, when the men compare notes, each of them insists that he alone understands what an elephant is like: his comrades are totally mistaken.

So, we told our students in the 1990s, each biblical approach or method yields some valid insight into "the meaning of the Bible" (or into "the mystery of divine revelation" or into "what God wants to say to us"). But we would be wise to listen to those whose experience with the Bible is different from ours.

The Insights series is born of humility: its very existence is testimony to our commitment that we need to compare notes about the Bible with openness to each other's diverse perspectives. But, beyond that, I would hope that these volumes might also lead us to admit the limits of our perception. We now see, as the apostle Paul puts it, "in a mirror dimly" (1 Cor 13:12)

Many, including myself, who study the Bible believe it is the word of God, meaning it is a source of divine revelation. For this reason alone, the meaning of the Bible is abundant and ubiquitous.

We probably understand the Bible here and now better than any other people in history, and this triumph has brought us to the realization of how little we can understand, now or ever. But, insights? Yes. Those we can claim. Our experiences, our knowledge, and our perspectives do have authenticity and from them we have at least gained some *insights* into the meaning of Scripture. Time to compare notes!

MARK ALLAN POWELL

Abbreviations

ABD   David Noel Freedman, Editor. *The Anchor Bible Dictionary*. New York: Doubleday, 1992.

BA   *Biblical Archaeologist*

BAR   *Biblical Archaeology Review*

BASOR   *Bulletin of the American Schools of Oriental Research*

Bib   *Biblica*

Byz.   Byzantine

EB   Early Bronze

ER   Early Roman

Hell.   Hellenistic

IDB   George Arthur Buttrick, Editor. *The Interpreter's Dictionary of the Bible*. Nashville: Abingdon, 1962.

IDB (New)   Katharine Doob Sakenfeld, Editor. *The New Interpreter's Dictionary of the Bible*. Nashville: Abingdon, 2006–2009.

IEJ   *Israel Exploration Journal*

IJO   *International Journal of Osteoarchaeology*

JBL   *Journal of Biblical Literature*

JRA   *Journal of Roman Archaeology*

JSOT   *Journal for the Study of the Old Testament*

LB   Late Bronze

LR   Late Roman

MB   Middle Bronze

MR	Middle Roman
NEA	*Near Eastern Archaeology*
NovT	*Novum Testamentum*
NTS	*New Testament Studies*
OEANE	Eric M. Meyers, Editor. *The Oxford Encyclopedia of Archaeology in the Near East.* New York: Oxford, 1997.
PEQ	*Palestine Exploration Quarterly*
PJ	*Palästina Jahrbuch*
RevExp	*Review and Expositor*
RevQ	*Revue de Qumran*
TZ	*Theologische Zeitschrift*

Preface

Archaeology! The very word sounds exciting. We picture Indiana Jones in his dashing outfit (inexplicably carrying a bullwhip!), robbing tombs of priceless museum pieces and enduring threats to his life in the process. How exciting! Many of us dream of such a career.

The truth is, archaeology is usually slow, painstaking, and hot labor. It may take years before archaeologists find "anything good" at a site. I have never met anyone in the field that even remotely reminded me of Harrison Ford (except for myself, of course). Robbing tombs is illegal. Most of the "museum pieces" found in Israel are rather homely and plain.

Yet archaeology can be exciting if the excitement is about the people whose lives we come to know through the remains. If you expect to see your picture in the *New York Times* standing with a serious and scholarly expression on your face, surrounded by smiling "locals," while you modestly point toward your sensational discovery under the screaming headlines: "HOW I FOUND THE ARK OF THE COVENANT!"—you may want to explore another career or at least another venue for your career. That will almost never happen in Israel.

If, however, meeting ancient folk through "their stuff" excites you, you might want to consider archaeology as a career or hobby. If you can hold a broken cooking pot, reflect on the ancient hands that fashioned it from wet clay, imagine the persons that handled the pot repeatedly to cook meals, and finally picture in your mind's eye the many hands—large and small—that dipped into the pot to eat, then you will love archaeology. The artifacts tell us about the people who used them. That is where the "excitement" lies.

Yet my task in this small volume is not to entice anyone to grab a trowel and start digging willy-nilly—please do not do that—but to introduce the reader to the ways archaeology can assist in biblical interpretation. It clearly does help in the task. Although not all archaeologists and biblical scholars agree on precisely how the material remains give us interpretative insights, there is a rough consensus. I will, I hope, help the reader to see why these conclusions make sense.

One observation should be clear, if not now, then I hope by the end of your reading this monograph: to ignore the results of archaeology is unwise. Old Testament scholars have known this for a century or more; New Testament interpreters are beginning to understand this as well. The old excuse—"I am a text woman/text man, I don't do archaeology"—will no longer hold. Everyone needs to "do archaeology" in the sense that the material remains are considered. While actual excavation experience is not yet a requisite to become a good biblical interpreter, some reading about the results of archaeology should be required of everyone earning a degree in Biblical Studies.

I hope in chapter 1 to set the table for our feast. Here I intend to survey the common suggestions as to how one can and should use archaeology. Of course, there have been abuses and misuses in the past one hundred or more years, but today there seem to be four or five commonly used approaches in the proper use of material remains in interpreting the Bible.

Chapter 2 will offer the reader some concrete examples of the suggestions of chapter 1. We will look at some of the great events of the Old Testament and at some of the unexpected discoveries relating to the New Testament that both expand and confirm our knowledge of certain narratives. But once a person dips his or her toe into the waters of archaeology, he or she must be prepared for occasional discomfort as well. Some of the remains appear to contradict (or at least challenge) the historicity of the biblical narratives. Not all of the discoveries offer "sensational confirmation" of the Bible. Some present us with "sensational contradictions" of the Bible.

Chapter 3 will lead the reader on a sustained tour through an Iron Age (i.e., Old Testament period) Israelite house. In walking through a family's house and inspecting their furnishings like a group of tourists, we will also have occasion to speak briefly about the nature of the Israelite family based on what we learn from their houses. I hope to create on paper a fictional Israelite family and guide the reader through a typical day in their lives.

Chapter 4 will seek to pull together many publications on the skeletal remains from the Second Temple Period in Israel, that is, the period of the Jesus Movement and the Gospels. As we will see in chapter 1 of this volume, one of the goals in studying the material remains of Israel is to reconstruct the *social* world of the people. But in chapter 4, I hope to contribute toward reconstructing a bit of the *personal* world of the people. What was it like for individuals personally to live in New Testament–era Israel? This chapter will be rather like a sad stroll through cemeteries to ponder the brevity of life.

Chapter 5 provides in summary fashion a reminder of what archaeology can and cannot do. Archaeology cannot be used to prove or disprove the Bible, and it cannot tell us all we want to know about the biblical world. It also cannot tell us if the Bible is right or true (theologically). Archaeology can help us reconstruct the social, economic, household, and material environment of the world in which the Bible was written. It can even, occasionally, shed light on a biblical text with the effect of changing the interpretation of a specific text. Finally, it can offer confirmation (or contradiction) of a text, event, or person of the Bible.

No research today can or should be done without the consultation of others. I wish to thank Carol Meyers, Eric Meyers, and Dennis Groh for kindly reading portions of this monograph and offering helpful suggestions. Yet, they can only give advice; it is up to me to take it. Thus any remaining weaknesses are, of course, my own.

Most importantly, I wish to thank my wife, Molly, for her continued friendship and partnership in life's endeavors and challenges, without whom projects like this one would be much less enjoyable.

1

Vocational Guidance Counseling: What Archaeology Is and What Archaeologists Do

Archaeology, simply put, is "the scientific study of material remains of past human life and activities."[1] Or, put a little more expansively, it is the "recovery, classification, and description of the material remains of antiquity."[2] Archaeology is "another kind of research . . . the research [that] focuses not on texts . . . but rather on what we call 'material culture.'"[3] Or one could say that archaeology is a "way of making inferences about 'how it was in the past' by examining material culture remains . . . [it is an] ethnography of the dead."[4]

Well, those are formal definitions. In practical terms: archaeologists study "bits and pieces of other people's garbage,"[5] or they "[deal] with the wreckage of antiquity."[6] Archaeology focuses on what is left over

1. W. G. Dever, "Archaeology," 44. This definition is very similar to Hoppe, *Biblical Archaeology*, 3; and the official definition at the Archaeological Institute of America's website: "The scientific excavation and study of ancient human material remains" (No author, "Introduction to Archaeology").
2. Hoppe, *Biblical Archaeology*, 8.
3. Dever, *Biblical Writers*, 53.
4. Ibid., 54.
5. Ibid., 53.
6. G. E. Wright, "Archaeology," 76.

after wars, natural disasters, and time have had their effects. Obviously, only the most durable objects (stone, fired clay, metal, and bones) survive with any regularity, although sometimes more perishable treasures are found—such as cloth, texts written on animal skins or papyri, or wooden objects—if the climate allows it.

We might distinguish the following categories in archaeology:

1. written remains (on clay, stone, pottery pieces, papyrus, or vellum);
2. nonwritten remains, including (a) large structures (such as fortifications, gates, religious buildings, and domestic structures) and (b) small finds (such as jewelry, weapons, coins, pottery, bones, and glass).[7] We will be dealing with all three categories of remains in this work.

Fig. 1.1 Excavation to bedrock. Shikhin Excavation Project. Used with permission.

First, let me state up front that this is not a "how to" manual. We will not review the process of excavation in this volume. Previous introductions have done this,[8] and anyway, it is difficult to get a clear picture

---

7. See Lance, *Old Testament*, 5 who lists only two categories; and Gibson, *Cave of John the Baptist*, 3 who lists all three.
8. The introductions and manuals for archaeology are legion. See the classic descriptions of excavation by Albright, *Archaeology*, 7–22; Badè, *Manual*; and Kenyon, *Beginning*, 68–144. For more recent descriptions, see Mazar, *Archaeology*, 1–34; McRay, *Archaeology*, 20–34. More popularly, one can

of what happens on a dig without doing one. This volume will present ways biblical scholars and archaeologists have used archaeology to understand the Bible. In engaging in this task, we will in this chapter poll several scholars' general guidelines for the interaction of biblical texts and archaeology. We will observe that they agree, in the main, about the appropriate uses of archaeology in interpreting the Bible.

Second, let me say that I am not an archaeologist. I have participated in a number of archaeological excavations and surveys, but that does not make one an archaeologist. I have read widely in the field but that does not qualify me either. So, then, what is an archaeologist? William Dever defines an archaeologist as one "who writes history from things."[9] But that definition does not tell us enough.

Fig. 1.2 Excavation in progress. Photograph by the author.

look at Lance, *Old Testament*, 22–35; and Hoppe, *Biblical Archaeology*, 13–33. For a survey of archaeology handbooks, see Dessel, "Good Book." For a detailed description of excavation technique and procedures, see: Strange et al., *Excavations at Shikhin*; no author, *Tel Gezer Excavation Manual*; and Herr and Christopherson, *Excavation Manual*. For a brief video that explains the digging process, see No Author, "The Excavation Process."

9. Dever, *Biblical Writers*, 53.

In my experiences on excavations, I have discerned four levels of participants to whom people sometimes assign the title "archaeologist." The *first level* I call the "dirt movers." These are the grunts—I have been one of them on numerous excavations—who actually dig up the dirt and move it to the dump pile. To be sure, they dig in an orderly and planned way, but they mostly dig, move, and dump. Along the way they collect artifacts: potsherds, bones, coins, jewelry, glass, tesserae, bricks, metal instruments, weapons, and household items such as door keys, stone vessels, loom weights, spindle whorls, and lamps. Sometimes they use a pick (or a small pick called a *patish*), sometimes a brush, but most of the time they use a trowel. The emphasis is on moving dirt without damaging the artifacts below while remaining observant of stratigraphy. Thus, diggers are cautioned to be on the lookout for breakable ceramics and glass and for changes in the soil. The recovered artifacts are then turned over to the next level of "archaeologists."

The *second level* I call the "recorders." These folk might be the square supervisors who take notes, sketch top plans, and draw balks. They take daily elevations and measure large objects such as pieces of plaster, pieces of brick, stones, and stoneware vessels. Or, other recorders might be those who receive the artifacts from the dirt movers. The smaller artifacts are placed in boxes or envelopes, labeled, and then given to the artifact recorder(s). These persons might not even visit the site but remain back at the base camp—perhaps a hotel room—and record, package, and store artifacts. Recorders might also include those with certain specialties such as surveying. The work of the recorders is essential for those coming later in levels three and four. They work not with a trowel but with a notebook.

The *third level* I name the "interpreters." They "read" the artifacts, whether potsherds, coins, lamp fragments, or other finds. They want to assign a date and function to the artifact. For example, a rim of a ceramic ware might tell the interpreter that the vessel was manufactured in the Iron II[10] period and that it was a storage vessel. A numismatist might determine that a coin was Hasmonean.

---

10. For the dates of these assignations, see the appendix of this volume, based on A. Mazar, *Archaeology*, 30 (for Neolithic-Iron age dates) and Fiensy and Strange, *Galilee I*, ix (for Persian-Islamic dates).

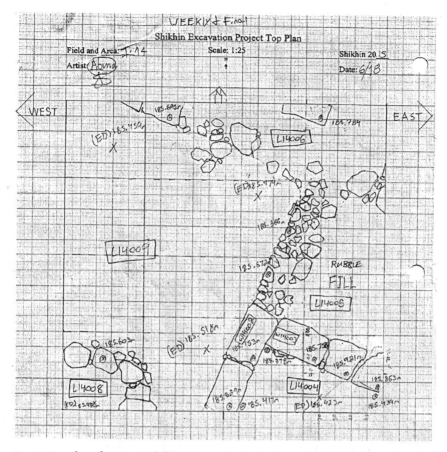

Fig. 1.3 Top plan of a square. Shikhin Excavation Project. Used with permission.

A bone expert might determine that certain bones were from sheep. If one has excavated a tomb and collected human bones, a physical anthropologist would tell the age, sex, and general condition of the person at death. An expert in ancient weaponry might decide that an arrowhead was Roman. An architect might inspect the standing ruins of buildings. The interpreters are experts in their fields of interpretation. No single person knows about all of these areas, though sometimes those in the next level of archaeology will also be an expert interpreter in one of them (usually in pottery).

One might also include in this level the restorers of material remains. Most commonly, these are persons who piece together potsherds (or pieces of glass) into an original vessel (or part of it) in order to understand more completely the vessel's function. A restorer also might produce a sketch of the original vessel or artifact. A restorer is a kind of interpreter of the remains, since she or he is presenting to the public what the vessel looked like in the first place.

Fig. 1.4 Potsherds excavated and washed. Shikhin Excavation Project. Used with permission.

Fig. 1.5 Pottery "reading." Shikhin Excavation Project. Used with permission.

Fig. 1.6 Middle Roman–era jar, partially restored. Photograph by the author.

Fig. 1.7 Partially reconstructed house from the MR-LR village of Katzrin. Photograph by the author.

Others might restore part of a building by repositioning stones now lying on the ground into their original places. By so doing, the restorers want visitors to the site to gain a better understanding of the building's original appearance and function. Such restorations of buildings are also, of course, interpretations. On the one hand, they seek to clarify what the material remains represent. But on the other hand, they can mislead if the interpreter misunderstands the object.

The *fourth level* of archaeological participant is the "director." This is the person (usually the dig director) who will—often assisted by his/her colleagues, perhaps named associate directors—put it all together for a coherent picture of the site. These are the people who "(write) history from things." This person will seek to understand the site in all its levels of occupation and in the context of its geography and chronology. This person must be familiar with the political, economic, and cultural history of the region. She must be able to envision the big picture. The director must see the village or building as it was through successive periods of time. He must understand how this site related economically, politically, and culturally with its surroundings. Succeeding in this synthesis is only possible if the recorders and interpreters have done their job adequately.

So which of these persons should we dub an "archaeologist"? Certainly the fourth level qualifies as a real archaeologist, and I would say possibly the third level if someone devotes his or her skill mostly to archaeology.[11] But the first and second levels would not qualify in my opinion. That is why I say that, although I have participated on levels one and two, it does not make me an archaeologist.

Further—let me add respectfully—not every archaeologist (i.e., those on the "director's" level) is necessarily also a good historian/biblical exegete or one who "writes [good] history from things";[12] some seem unable to go beyond extracting and interpreting artifacts and then writing these interpretations up in the final report. They are enormously skilled at conceiving of the excavation queries, organizing the dig, and then synthesizing all of the data into a narrative. But integrating their excavation narrative into the flow of history—interpreting or reinterpreting history because of it—does not always happen. But the best ones are also good historians who can then integrate the material findings of their excavation into the larger historical picture and even, as a result, expand our knowledge of the history of a people.

11. But is a chemist, for example, who occasionally takes Carbon 14 or neutron activation analyses of items an archaeologist? Is an expert in ancient glass or bones an archaeologist?
12. See Hoppe, *Biblical Archaeology*, 6: "[T]he archaeologist is neither an exegete nor an historian." This statement may be a bit exaggerated. Some archaeologists are also good historians and/or exegetes. Cf. the statement of Eric Meyers: "Not everyone can be a good biblical scholar and an excellent field archaeologist at the same time" (Meyers, "Bible and Archaeology," 2006: lxi).

The Modern Context for the Study of "Biblical Archaeology"[13]

No discipline exists in a vacuum; it is informed not only by its current environment but also by its heritage. The archaeological investigation of material remains that relate to the Bible has a history that drives much of what is happening today. Thus it is helpful, in getting our bearings, to review briefly the history of the Biblical Archaeology movement in the United States.

Phase I

The use of archaeology to assist in biblical studies—to serve as the handmaid of biblical studies—reached its "Golden Age" from the 1920s to the 1960s.[14] In this period, "Biblical Archaeology" was a subdiscipline under biblical studies, and this approach to the use of archaeology dominated American Palestinian archaeological excavations.[15] It existed to serve, illuminate, and prove the Bible (especially the Old Testament). During those years William F. Albright's influence was at its peak. He appears to have had an agenda from the start for his use of archaeology in biblical studies. Albright believed that archaeology could verify the historicity of the biblical texts. He wanted both to prove the Bible and to oppose German higher criticism. He could write in 1957, after decades of excavating:

> I defend the substantial historicity of patriarchal tradition, without any appreciable change in my point of view . . . I have not surrendered a single position with regard to early Israelite monotheism but . . . consider the Mosaic tradition as even more reliable than I did then (in 1940) . . . I have grown more conservative in my attitude to Mosaic tradition.[16]

Albright's excavations—and those of his numerous PhD students—were for the purpose of establishing the historical trustworthiness of the Old Testament. Yet, in spite of his tendentiousness, he and his students and

---

13. For this section, see Killebrew, "Heaven and Earth"; Laughlin, "Convergence"; Dever, *Biblical Writers*, 1–21; E. Meyers, "Bible and Archaeology" (1984); idem., "Bible and Archaeology" (2006); Finkelstein and Silberman, *Bible Unearthed*, 21–24; Levy, "New Pragmatism"; Davis, "Faith"; Bunimovitz and Faust, "Re-constructing"; Garroway, *Children*, 26–30; and Zangenberg, "Archaeology and the New Testament."
14. Garroway, *Children*, 26 divides Phase I into three periods: before World War I, between the wars, and post–World War II (until the 1970s). She assigns the second period (between the wars) the title the "Golden Age" of archaeology.
15. See Dever, "Biblical Archaeology," 315.
16. Albright, *Stone Age*, 2.

protégés—most famously G. E. Wright and Nelson Glueck—produced some groundbreaking work in archaeology.

Phase II

But in the 1960s and 1970s a new paradigm emerged to challenge Albright. Though initiated by G. E. Wright,[17] one of Wright's students, William Dever,[18] intensified the call for a separation of biblical studies from the yoke of "Biblical Archaeology." He wanted to secularize the discipline and to rename it "Syro-Palestinian" archaeology. He and others wanted to study the material remains in their own right with reference to anthropology rather than to biblical studies. They saw archaeology not as the handmaiden of biblical studies but as its own discipline. Dever lists the following reasons for the demise of Biblical Archaeology: "amateurish fieldwork . . . parochial character . . . reactionary nature . . . resistance to growing trends toward specialization . . . [and failure] to achieve its own major objective [i.e. demonstrate the historicity of the Bible]."[19]

Dever himself identifies both external and internal factors that resulted in the paradigm shift. The main external factor was the influence of American New World archaeology, which emphasized anthropology—an emphasis that remains today (see chapter 3)—over history, which sought to study the processes of cultural changes (hence processualist), and which was multidisciplinary in method (using several of the sciences). Internal changes included the stratigraphic insights of Kathleen Kenyon and what Dever terms "a more professional" approach to the discipline.[20]

The "New Archaeology" of this period has been called "a-historical, even anti-historical."[21] It wanted to remove the connection between the Bible and the material remains. It began to see its task more as an anthropological one rather than a historical one; it wanted to study culture and culture change, not attempt to demonstrate the historicity of the Old Testament. It was, according to Dever, much more attuned

---

17. See E. Meyers, "Bible and Archaeology," 1984: 37.
18. Although Dever denies that he "killed" the Biblical Archaeology movement, apparently not all would agree: "By the early 1970s I ventured to say in print what many had sensed: that Biblical archaeology as an academic discipline was dead. I did not kill it, as some have claimed. I'm flattered, but in truth I simply observed its passing and wrote its obituary." Dever, *Recent Archaeological*, 22.
19. Dever, *Biblical Writers*, 58.
20. Dever, "Biblical Archaeology," 316–17.
21. Bunimovitz and Faust, "Re-constructing," 45.

to stratigraphic concerns and much more insistent on an interdisci-plinary approach to the task, utilizing geologists, botanists, zoologists, and chemists, among others.[22] Further, about this same time, many of the excavations and surveys began to challenge the historicity of the Old Testament. The certainty that archaeology could defend the patri-archal narratives, the exodus, and even the Israelite monarchy was being undermined. Thus, the house of Albright began to crumble.

Coincidentally with this movement arose the minimalist/maximalist debate. The minimalists declared that very little if anything in the Old Testament was of historical value. The Old Testament was written in the Persian, Hellenistic, and even in the Roman periods. It is a late com-position and has no value for the study of the Iron Age in Israel. They were the polar opposite to Albright's confident use of archaeology to demonstrate the Old Testament's historical reliability.[23]

We might also note that coincidental with the new paradigm in Old Testament archaeology and biblical studies was the development of New Testament archaeology as a discipline. There had been previous excavations in Jerusalem and Capernaum by the Franciscans and oth-ers and at sites in Greece and Asia Minor,[24] but in the 1970s a new and organized impetus began in Galilee in Israel. At the instigation of G. E. Wright, Eric Meyers (another of his students) and his colleagues, James F. Strange and Dennis Groh, led a team to survey and to begin excavating in Galilee, home to both early Christianity and reformu-lated Judaism after the great war of 66–73 CE. This initiative, called the Meiron Excavation Project, was the foundation for the modern "archaeology of early Judaism and Christianity."[25] Thus the field of New Testament archaeology (and its partner the archaeology of early Judaism) is rather a latecomer in comparison with the archaeology of the Hebrew Bible.[26] Most of the debate over the Bible and archae-ology and the development of methodology have so far taken place with respect to the Hebrew Bible, with the New Testament interpreters

---

22. Dever, *Biblical Writers*, 59.
23. See ibid., 23–52.
24. See Zangenberg, "Archaeology and the New Testament."
25. E. Meyers, "New Testament and Archaeology." Meyers comments that the early 1970s were "the beginning of a new era for New Testament archaeology."
26. Zangenberg: "Only when New Testament scholars became not simply recipients but producers of prime data and partners in dialogue should one speak of New Testament archaeology. In this respect New Testament archaeology is a fairly recent development, even though it continued a much older impulse . . ." ("Archaeology and the New Testament," lxiii).

trailing at some distance behind their Old Testament colleagues.[27] Meyers and his team have done much to begin to close the gap.

Phase III

This phase began when, ironically, Dever himself realized he had taken the secularization of Syro-Palestinian archaeology too far. Dever "realized that the total split between the two fields was more than he bargained for."[28] One of Dever's former students writes of this shift:

> I believe Dever's rejection of Biblical archaeology was initially a theological reaction. Like many new converts, Dever initially overstated his case, contending that objectivity was a problem only for theologians, that Biblical archaeology was a meaningless term and that the endeavor was amateurish in the extreme.[29]

Dever now reasoned that the Old Testament—interpreted critically—must be considered in any reconstruction of the Iron Age. He has recently argued forcefully—and against the minimalists' school—that Israelite history as related in the Old Testament is essentially historical with reference to the Iron II Age.[30] He characterizes himself as neither a "maximalist nor a minimalist," but he now defends a "historical core" of the Old Testament.[31]

Phase IV

Since the turn of the new millennium we are in the "historical Biblical Archaeology" (some say "post-processual"[32]) period. It seems now that all hands on deck want to distance themselves from both Albright's and Dever's agendas. This movement seeks to let archaeology speak for itself without the Old Testament asking the questions, but still wants to allow the Old Testament to be at the center of the investigation by reading it as a cultural document. There is also great interest in using

---

27. Dever noted in 1997: "Biblical archaeology has been almost exclusively the province of scholars of the Hebrew Bible . . ." ("Biblical Archaeology," 319).
28. Bunimovitz and Faust, "Re-constructing," 47.
29. Davis, "Faith," 58.
30. Dever, *Biblical Writers*, 23–52.
31. Ibid., 267–70, 297.
32. For a definition of Processual archaeology, see Levy, "New Pragmatism," 5; Dever, *Biblical Writers*, 59; and Krijgsman, "Biblical Studies." Krijgsman ("Biblical Studies," 6) calls it the "post-processual" period. Garroway, *Children*, 28 maintains that we are now in the "Processual-Plus" era, having passed the Post-Processual period. Eric Meyers and Carol Meyers call it "socio-archaeology" (E. Meyers, "Bible and Archaeology," 2006: lxi).

the latest scientific information in dating, especially in C^{14} dating techniques. Thomas Levy has called for a "New Pragmatism" in archaeology in which scholars "solve problems by transcending partisanship to foster cooperation."[33] For Levy a pragmatic approach means using a wide range of resources to form what he calls "historical Biblical Archaeology," including anthropology, biblical studies, scientific analytical fields, telecommunications, and information technology.[34]

Thus in our survey below, the stress will be on allowing archaeology to inform our knowledge of the environment or of the cultural context of the Bible. The old drive to prove the Bible or establish its historicity by appeal to the material remains is just about gone. But there is at the same time great interest in having archaeology interact with both the Hebrew Bible and the New Testament in the mutual interpretation of text and artifact. For, as some have noticed,[35] both words and artifacts are windows into worldviews.

General Guidelines for Using Archaeology to Interpret the Bible

In the remainder of this chapter, I will survey several scholars' general guidelines as to how a student of the Bible might benefit from the knowledge of archaeology. These are scholars who have for years reflected on the task of connecting archaeology with biblical interpretation. In chapter 2, I will give examples from both the Hebrew Bible and the New Testament for some of these uses.

Eric Meyers and co-author James F. Strange have offered four ways archaeology can be helpful in interpreting texts:

First, archaeology may supplement the ancient (textual) record by providing information not in the texts. The example they give is some of the excavations of synagogues in Israel. Much of the data on how synagogues were operated and built are not in the ancient texts. So, the excavations have greatly expanded our knowledge.

Second, archaeology may clarify a text. The example they give is the excavations of Jewish burials, which help us to understand both the Mishnah and the burial of Jesus as reported in the New Testament.

Third, archaeology might contradict a text. For example, although the rabbinic work called the Tosephta indicates that all synagogues were built on hilltops, it was not the case as the synagogue ruins now

33. Levy, "New Pragmatism," 9.
34. Ibid.
35. Bunimovitz and Faust, "Re-constructing," 43.

demonstrate. Also, Meyers and Strange point out, there is no village ruin approximately sixty stades from Jerusalem that might qualify as the village of Emmaus (Luke 24:13).

Finally, archaeology can confirm the historicity of a text. For example, synagogue excavations, they maintain, confirm the textual affirmation that they were built oriented toward Jerusalem.[36] As we will see below, these four uses are now standard and will guide our discussion in chapter 2.

J. H. Charlesworth[37] suggests three categories for using archaeology in the study of the historical Jesus. One category (which he names the "tertiary level") is comprised of any artifact that pertains to the background of Jesus. That is, this category refers to any object dating from Jesus's time that can help capture for us what it was like to live then. A second category (secondary level) includes material remains that describe the foreground of Jesus. These are remains that relate with some probability to the life of Jesus. Charlesworth lists, e.g., the town of Capernaum and its architectural and other material remains. We know from the Gospels that Jesus was in Capernaum, so learning more about this town may help us to understand the historical Jesus, suggests Charlesworth. The final category (primary level) includes "data from some period of the life of Jesus" such as the place of his crucifixion. This level focuses on a known event in his life (and evidently at a specific location). Thus, we move from the general toward the more specific.

Leslie J. Hoppe lists six ways people attempt to use archaeology (three of them inappropriate). Some use archaeology as treasure hunting, some to reinforce political agendas, and others to prove the Bible.[38] These are inappropriate uses of archaeology in Hoppe's judgment. Others use archaeology to clarify the biblical text, to "confirm the reliability of certain types of information provided by the [biblical] text," and to supplement the text with additional information. These last three uses Hoppe seems to approve of.[39]

Scott Starbuck has offered four outcomes "of integration of Near Eastern archaeology and biblical studies."[40] His four outcomes are very

---

36. Meyers and Strange, *Archaeology, the Rabbis, and Early Christianity*, 28–29. See also E. Meyers's more recent application of these four uses of archaeology in interpreting a text in his "Use of Archaeology."
37. Charlesworth, "Archaeology," 8–9.
38. For a recent interesting study of the improper uses of archaeology for nationalistic ends and to prove the Bible as historically true, see E. Meyers and C. Meyers, "Holy Land Archaeology."
39. Hoppe, *Biblical Archaeology*, 4–8.
40. Starbuck, "Things Forbidden?"

similar to Meyers and Strange's four ways listed above. Starbuck writes that Outcome 1, in integrating archaeology with biblical studies, is when the findings essentially confirm the biblical text. The example he gives of this outcome is the discovery of the House of David inscription (evidently confirming that David really lived in the Iron II period). Outcome 2 is when the archaeological discoveries expand our knowledge of the text or provide additional information beyond what the text gives us. His two examples of Outcome 2 are the cherub throne on the Megiddo ivories and the first-century "Galilee Boat," which illustrate items mentioned in the biblical texts. So far, so good for most students of the Bible.

Fig. 1.8 The so-called Galilee Boat (full-scale model based on the ancient hull found in the mud along the shore of the Sea of Galilee). Photograph by the author.

But with Outcome 3 comes conflict between the archaeological finds and the biblical text. His example here is the correction that archaeology offers for the conquest narratives of Joshua and Judges (see chapter 2 of this volume). Likewise, Outcome 4 is when the archaeological findings "conflict with the assumed dogmatic perspectives." Here the example is the finds at Kuntillet 'Ajrud, which refer to "Yahweh and his Ashera" (see further below in chapter 2).[41]

41. Ibid., 100–101, 111–12.

The aforementioned James F. Strange,[42] sixteen years after his co-authored work with Eric Meyers, presented new perspectives on how to use archaeology in the study of the biblical world. Archaeological remains, he writes in 1997, can assist the historian to: 1) Illustrate an object (e.g., a cup). This is the "least useful theoretical" level for the study of archaeology; 2) Reconstruct a practice (e.g., covering the head or dining with an important person); and 3) Reconstruct the social world. This use of archaeology is, according to Strange, the most sophisticated theoretical level of investigation.

Jonathan Reed compares the use of archaeology by historians to working a crossword puzzle. Just as the puzzle has blanks to fill in, running both vertically and horizontally, so does the writing of history. The New Testament (we will say, the vertical blanks) and archaeology (the horizontal blanks) fill in the empty spaces, some of which overlap as in a puzzle.[43] Reed maintains that archaeology's main "contribution to the study of the historical Jesus research lies in its ability to reconstruct his social world."[44] In other words, most of the interpretative assistance archaeology offers to the scholar of the historical Jesus (and I would add to those studying the rest of the New Testament) is background information.[45] Reed names information about demographic issues, ethnicity, religion, economics, and agricultural practices as some of the background issues archaeology can clarify for the interpreter of the New Testament Gospels.[46] There is very little help, maintains Reed, in reconstructing an event or in interpreting specific verses of the New Testament. But, as we will see later, this is not always the case with using archaeology to interpret the Old Testament. There are more data pertaining to the Hebrew Bible that help the interpreter reconstruct events (or dismiss them as unhistorical).

John McRay lists four uses of archaeology in interpreting the New Testament. First, it enlightens our understanding of the geographical setting of the New Testament. Excavations at Jericho and Kursi, for example, help us understand the biblical text (how can Jesus be said to enter and exit Jericho while doing the same miracle?) and decide where a biblical event took place (Kursi as the place for the demoniac story). Second, archaeology helps us understand the religious environment. Here he points to two collections of literature, the one found in Egypt

---

42. James Strange, "Sayings of Jesus and Archaeology," 296–97.
43. Compare Hoppe, *Biblical Archaeology*, 3.
44. Reed, *Archaeology*, 18.
45. See also Dennis Groh, "American Field School," 147.
46. Reed, *Archaeology*, 19.

(Nag Hammadi texts) and the other found in Israel (Dead Sea Scrolls). Third, the ruins help to establish the historicity of certain places (Well of Jacob; Pool of Bethesda; Pool of Siloam) and persons (Pontius Pilate; Erastus; Quirinius). Fourth, the finds, especially the Egyptian papyri, help us reconstruct the New Testament Greek text.[47]

Lee Levine has offered three ways that the archaeological data can relate to the literary sources: Sometimes the archaeological finds confirm what we have read (at least our interpretations of what we have read) in the literature. He gives the excavations of Masada as an example of this usage. At other times, the archaeological data supplement the literary works. Archaeology offers more information that enables us to fill out what is in the written sources. He finds this use of archaeology in the excavations of urban centers. Third, archaeology can raise "new questions and issues." He suggests that the finds from Qumran and, to a lesser extent, Beth She'arim have done as much. These sites with their unexpected remains have revolutionized our understanding of the ancient Jewish world.[48]

Fig. 1.9 Façade of the Beth She'arim Tomb Complex. Photograph by the author.

William Dever also wrote in 1990 about four ways that archaeology can assist in understanding the biblical text. First, it helps create the historical and cultural context of the Bible. It "illustrates" the biblical

47. McRay, *Archaeology*, 17–19.
48. Levine, "Archaeological Discoveries," 76.

world: "Archaeology may not have proven the specific historical existence of certain Biblical personalities such as Abraham or Moses, but it has for all time demolished the notion that the Bible is pure mythology."[49] In other words, the material remains support the text in constructing the life and times of the Hebrew people if not always agreeing with the named events. Second, the material remains can help in understanding specific phrases or verses in the Hebrew Bible. Dever lists as examples the many newly clarified phrases and words in the Hebrew Psalms, made possible especially by the Ugaritic texts. One word in particular he lists is the Hebrew word פים found in 1 Samuel 13:19–31. We now know, based on the discovery of small stones with the inscription "pîm" in palaeo-Hebrew, that the word refers to a weight of 7.8 grams.[50] Third, the material remains can supply "missing elements of the story" (e.g., the siege and destruction of the city of Lachish; see chapter 2 below).[51] Fourth, the remains reveal "common everyday life of the average Israelite or Judean."[52]

Twenty-one years after his aforementioned 1990 essay, William Dever wrote more expansively about two ways in which archaeology can expand our understanding of a text of the Hebrew Bible. He termed these two ways "convergences" and "divergences." Convergences[53] are when references in the Hebrew Bible harmonize with nonbiblical data (inscriptions, artwork, and material remains such as pottery or buildings). Convergences happen when biblical texts and artifacts come together to support and explain one another.[54] For example, the Hebrew Bible describes early Israel (Iron I) as organized by households, tribes, and clans with endogamous marriage, patrilocal society and identity within the "father's house." The archaeological remains indicate a house plan and layout reflecting kin-based social structure, homogenous villages, and an economic structure betraying a "domestic mode of production."[55] In other words, the material remains are what one would expect for a society like that depicted in the Hebrew Bible.

Likewise, synchronisms, when biblical chronologies line up with similar events or persons elsewhere in the Ancient Near East,[56] form a

---

49. Dever, *Recent Archaeological*, 32.
50. Ibid., 33.
51. Ibid., 34.
52. Ibid., 35.
53. Dever, *Biblical Writers*, 83, 85, 91, 94, 106, 124–28, 131, 132, 160, 167, 208, 239, 240, 271; and Dever, *Ordinary People*, 99, 189–91.
54. Dever, *Biblical Writers*, 83.
55. Ibid., 125. Dever gives a list here of ten features that are paralleled in the Bible and in archaeology.

kind of convergence. For example, Dever gives a list of monarchs for the divided kingdoms of Israel and Judah (in the Iron II period) and a corresponding list of Mesopotamian monarchs. These "king lists" harmonize because many of the Israelite monarchs' names are given in the Mesopotamian literature.[57]

Dever argues that one must not only look for *convergences* but also for *divergences*.[58] He has used the "external data of archaeology" to isolate a reliable "historical core" of events narrated in the Old Testament. These reliable events enable Dever to construct a "*real* Israel in the Iron Age."[59] In other words, the "divergences" are places where archaeology seems to disagree with the biblical text and thus to correct the text. These two uses of archaeology—finding convergences and divergences—are highlighted by Dever in order to establish the essential historicity of Israel from the Iron Age. They have enabled him to "defend the middle ground"[60] in writing Israelite history. He is, therefore, as he maintains, neither a minimalist nor a maximalist.[61]

Finally, we give the suggestions in the helpful collection edited by Milton Moreland. The authors of the "Introduction" of this collection inform us of four ways that archaeology helps the biblical interpreter. First, archaeology allows us to "visualize the items, environments, and landscapes taken for granted in the texts." Second, archaeology helps us unfold "political and social motivations for events." Third, artifacts remind us of "voices left out of texts and alert us to biases." Fourth, archaeology can help create new knowledge that leads to a "richly textured set of historical reconstructions for the cultures of the biblical world."[62]

We can chart these ideas for using archaeology in the service of biblical interpretation as follows:

---

56. Ibid., 92, 137, 160, 162.
57. Ibid., 163.
58. Ibid., 271.
59. Ibid., 267.
60. Ibid., 297.
61. Cf. Laughlin, "Convergence."
62. Moreland, Burkes, and Aubin, "Introduction," 1–2. The collection was the result of a series of "consultations" conducted in Durham, NC and Eugene, OR in 2000–2001 (ibid., 6).

Use of archaeology	1	2	3	4	5	6	7	8	9	10
Illustrate/visualize		X			X			X		
Supplement the text	X		X	X			X	X	X	
Clarify the text	X		X					X		X
Contradict the text	X			X			X	X		
Confirm the text	X		X	X			X	X		X
Reconstruct the social/religious world		X			X	X		X	X	X
Reconstruct a practice					X					
Allow us to hear voices left out of the literature									X	
Reconstruct the biblical text										X
Treasure hunting				Y						
Reinforce political agendas				Y						
Prove the Bible				Y						

**Table 1.1 Illustration of how several scholars articulate
"how archaeology informs biblical study"**
(1 Meyers and Strange; 2 Charlesworth; 3 Hoppe; 4 Starbuck; 5 J. F. Strange;
6 Reed; 7 Levine; 8 Dever [2X]; 9 Moreland et al.; 10 McRay)
X= approved uses; Y= unapproved uses

As the reader can quickly see, these scholars essentially agree on the uses of archaeology in biblical interpretation, although some of them offer a unique perspective. The four uses offered by E. Meyers and J. F. Strange (shaded in the table along with the general "Reconstruct the Social World") capture the main cluster of suggestions. As a result, we will follow their outline in chapter 2 in our more extensive survey of examples of both archaeologists and biblical scholars using the material remains to interpret the text of the Bible. One more commonly cited use of archaeology—reconstructing the social world—will be the topic of both chapters 3 and 4.

A Step Beyond

As mentioned above, excavation skills do not always translate into historical skills. One might compose a plausible narrative about a site ("This site began in the Hellenistic II period, was expanded in the Early

Roman period, and was destroyed in the Middle Roman period") or of a building ("The building served in the Iron II period as an administrative center; in the Persian period as a storage building; and in the Hellenistic I period as a domestic dwelling") but not effectively integrate the finds into the larger historical record. Why was the site begun, expanded, and then destroyed? What was happening in the wider history that influenced the site's development? How does knowledge of this site change or refine our understanding of the wider history? For a helpful integration—or "conjunction"—of the material remains and the texts, one needs a larger plan, a method of history writing. One needs a way to integrate the material remains into the texts.

John Dominic Crossan has proposed such a method in his work on early Christianity. He sees his history writing as a three-stage task: He begins with "Context," which is based on a foundation of cross-cultural anthropology, followed by general Roman and Jewish history. On this basis he places "Lower Galilean Archeology." Next he turns to "Text" (made up of earliest, intermediate, and latest layers) and finally to "Conjunction," the linkage of context and text. His pictorial representation is as follows:

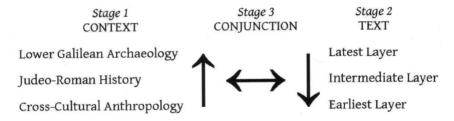

Stage 1 CONTEXT	*Stage 3* CONJUNCTION	*Stage 2* TEXT
Lower Galilean Archaeology		Latest Layer
Judeo-Roman History		Intermediate Layer
Cross-Cultural Anthropology		Earliest Layer

Table 1.2 Crossan's model of his historical method[63]

Crossan stresses that his method is interdisciplinary, interactive, and hierarchical. He is looking for "hard locks" between archaeological, anthropological, and textual data. Where do the three especially overlap and agree? Crossan further explains that this model is, and should be, flexible. That is, one must be free to "change, abandon, or replace" it as the data require.[64] But utilizing anthropology opens up the historian to new perspectives and takes her out of her familiar contemporary culture. Studying general history helps one place the material

---

63. Crossan, *Birth*, 147.
64. Ibid., 149.

remains into their broader background. In this way, Crossan's Context, his background to the Text (Bible), is an interactive exercise among the three considerations that in turn, as a synthesized whole, interact with the Text. Archaeology, in this model, has become one of the three components of Context. Although Crossan developed his model based on his Historical Jesus research, this approach seems to me fair and workable—with certain adaptations—for biblical research in general.

In chapters 3 and 4, I will attempt to place the material remains in such a model. We will ask what anthropological studies might contribute to our understanding of the material remains and how this anthropological and archaeological information can help interpret the texts as well as how the texts might in turn help us interpret the material remains. We will also place our archaeological and textual data into the broader context of the history of the Ancient Near East and the Greco-Roman Mediterranean world respectively. In chapter 3, we will refer to *cultural* anthropology (ethnographies) as an assistant; in chapter 4, we will vary a bit from Crossan's script and be informed by *physical* anthropology.

2

Digging Up the Bible: Examples of Using Archaeology to Interpret the Bible

Many of the suggestions from various authors given in chapter 1 overlap with those of their colleagues, as the table at the end of the chapter illustrates. Therefore, I will below merge several of these ideas together. My basic outline will follow the four uses presented by Meyers and Strange. Within this list I intend to incorporate a lengthy section on "clarifying" a text. I will divide the clarifying use of archaeology into Direct and Indirect clarification. It is the latter subsection that has been the most fruitful for the role of archaeology. Another term we might use instead of the moniker "Indirect clarification" is "background" or even "context." Most of the helpfulness of archaeology in interpreting the Bible is in providing background to the text.[1] In addition to the survey of examples of using archaeology in this chapter, I hope to add more in-depth examples in the succeeding two chapters.

Archaeology Supplements the Biblical Text

Let us offer an example from the Hebrew Bible and then one from the New Testament.

---

1. As Dennis Groh observes ("American Field School," 147).

Sennacherib's Invasion

In 701 BCE the Assyrian king, Sennacherib, invaded Judah, besieged Jerusalem, and conquered the town of Lachish. Both 2 Kings/Isaiah and 2 Chronicles give bits of information about the invasion. But now we can supplement the stories from the Hebrew Bible with two artifacts from Assyria and some remains from excavations and surveys of Israel:

1. The Sennacherib clay prism in cuneiform script containing the report of his invasion;
2. The *bas* relief sculpture that depicts the assault and conquest of the Judahite city of Lachish (see panel 7 of this sculpture below);
3. The archaeological excavations of Lachish itself;
4. The excavations and surveys of the area surrounding Lachish.

First, we look at the so-called Sennacherib Prism, which narrates his invasion.

2 Kings 18:13–14 / Isaiah 36:1	2 Chronicles 32:9	Sennacherib Prism
In the fourteenth year of Hezekiah, Sennacherib invaded Judah and besieged its fortified cities . . . Hezekiah sent a message to Sennacherib at Lachish.	Sennacherib sends messengers to Jerusalem while he is still besieging Lachish.	Sennacherib invades Judah and conquers forty-six walled cities and innumerable villages, capturing a host of people and animals as booty.

The clay prism containing the annals of Sennacherib gives a rather detailed account of his "third invasion." It narrates that Sennacherib conquered coastal cities such as Sidon, Tyre, Akko, and Ashkelon; then he came to Judah. In the course of describing his conquest of Judah, the prism refers to Hezekiah by name three times. The annals say that Sennacherib besieged forty-six walled cities and many villages, that he displaced 200,150 persons, and that he took as booty thirty talents of gold, 800[2] talents of silver (2 Kgs 18:14–17 says Hezekiah paid thirty talents of gold and 300 talents of silver), precious stones, ivory, ebony, and even some of Hezekiah's daughters and concubines.[3]

We read further in the Old Testament texts that Sennacherib surrounded Hezekiah in Jerusalem, that Hezekiah had to pay him off with

---

2. So reads the translation of Pritchard, *Texts*, 1.200 of the cuneiform inscription on the prism of Sennacherib. But Ussishkin, *Biblical Lachish*, used the translation of D. Winton Thomas, which says that Hezekiah paid Sennacherib 300 talents of silver, the same as the biblical text.

3. Pritchard, *Texts*, 1.199–201.

huge sums of gold, and that something curious happened to the Assyrians (a plague?) causing them to withdraw from Jerusalem.[4] The annals brag that Sennacherib shut up Hezekiah in Jerusalem "like a bird in a cage" but do not indicate that Sennacherib conquered Jerusalem. A story in the history of the Greek author Herodotus may also be related to this event. Herodotus wrote that when the Assyrians besieged "Egypt," swarms of mice ate their bowstrings and quivers and made it impossible for the Assyrians to attack.

2 Kings 19:20–36	Sennacherib prism	Herodotus, *History* 2.141–42
Sennacherib laid siege to Jerusalem. Hezekiah prayed to YHWH; he answered Hezekiah through Isaiah; and the death angel that night killed 180,000 Assyrians.	Sennacherib shut up Hezekiah in Jerusalem, "like a bird in a cage."[5]	Assyria invaded Egypt (=Israel?). The king went into a shrine to complain to the god. He fell asleep and the god appeared to him in a dream. The god promised he would protect him. That night thousands of mice invaded the Assyrians and ate their bowstrings, quivers, and leather shields.

Most revealing, however, is the *bas* relief sculpture of the siege of Lachish that was placed in Sennacherib's royal palace in Nineveh. The sculpture in room XXXVI of the palace consists of twelve panels[6] that depict three scenes from the siege and conquest of the fortified town.[7] On the relief sculpture (see p. 29) we can see Assyrian soldiers attempting to scale the walls by a siege ramp, Judahites shooting arrows down from towers, captured men being flayed alive outside the walls, men, women, and children being led away into captivity, and men being impaled on long poles.[8] The sculpture puts a face on the invasion.

The three scenes depict: first, the lead-up to the attack; second, the assault of the city; and third, the aftermath of the conquest when some people and goods are led away to Nineveh and others are executed. David Ussishkin believes that the three men impaled (see photo below) were the governor of the city and his high-ranking officials.[9] Certainly, this interpretation conforms with what the clay prism of the annals of

4. See 2 Kings 19:35; 2 Chronicles 32:21–22; and Herodotus, *History* 2.141–42.
5. Translation in Pritchard, *Texts*, 1.200.
6. The reader can see all twelve panels in Ussishkin, *Conquest*, 76–131.
7. Ussishkin, *Biblical Lachish*, 329–34.
8. See Pritchard, *Texts*, 1.101–2. For an interpretation of the relief sculpture, see Barnett, "Siege of Lachish"; Uehlinger, "Clio in a World of Pictures"; and Ussishkin, *Biblical Lachish*, 334–49. Ussishkin thinks the relief sculpture is an accurate representation of the siege. Uehlinger believes the sculpture was made just a few months after the siege ended (222).
9. Ussishkin, *Biblical Lachish*, 340–41.

Sennacherib describe as the fate of the officials of Ekron: "I assaulted Ekron and killed the officials and patricians who had committed the crime and hung their bodies on poles."[10] The depiction of men, women, and children being led toward Nineveh as captives would fit what the annals say about the survivors of Ekron: the magistrates were impaled, the minor criminals were taken as prisoners of war, and the rest were simply let go.[11] If those sorts of things happened at all of the forty-six towns in Judah that Sennacherib conquered, it was a year of unspeakable terror for the Hebrew people.

The biblical story gives us at most only a hint of that kind of event. As Dever[12] points out, there are passing references in 2 Kings and Isaiah to Sennacherib's having been to Lachish, with 2 Chronicles referring briefly to a siege. The Prism of Sennacherib and the relief sculpture from Nineveh add considerably to our knowledge of the events and our appreciation of what it meant to be conquered by the Assyrians. The archaeological remains, then, expand on or supplement the biblical text.

Further, the excavations at Lachish support what the Assyrian finds tell us. Ussishkin's thorough report can guide us in the archaeological discoveries at Lachish itself. Ussishkin identifies Level III as the occupation level that Sennacherib destroyed. He opines that the city at this time had a civilian population in addition to its military/official occupants. Both the *bas* relief (men, women, and children being led into captivity) and the domestic buildings excavated at Lachish confirm this conclusion. The population of Lachish at this time was between 1,800 and 3600 persons.[13]

There is evidence of a siege ramp at Lachish. They excavated Assyrian military helmets and other armor. There were 850 iron arrowheads as well as many sling stones found. Archaeologists found mass graves (1500 individuals[14]) and an increase in pig bones at the time of the siege (indicating non-Hebrews in the area).[15] Level III of Lachish was clearly destroyed by a great conflagration. Even the bricks in the walls were changed by the intense heat. Ussishkin writes, "I do not recall any

---

10. Translation in Pritchard, *Texts*, 1.200.
11. Ibid.
12. Dever, *Biblical Writers*, 168. See 2 Kings 18:14, 17; 19:8 (//Isa 36:2; 37:8); and 2 Chronicles 32:9. Ussishkin, *Biblical Lachish*, 271 maintains that Micah chapter 1 also had Lachish in view.
13. Ussishkin, *Biblical Lachish*, 215, 323.
14. The burial could be from an earlier occupation. See the discussion in Ussishkin, *Biblical Lachish*, 319.
15. Dever, *Biblical Writers*, 168–69; Ussishkin, *Biblical Lachish*, 308–11.

other ancient site in the Land of Israel where devastation of such magnitude can be seen."[16]

Fig. 2.1 Siege of Lachish, the seventh of twelve panels from the palace of Sennacherib: In the center, one can see the gate of the city, the siege ramp, and two battering rams. Also, people are led away to captivity. In the lower right three men are impaled. Photograph in Pritchard, *Pictures*, photograph 373. Used with permission of Princeton University Press.

Further, the excavations and surveys elsewhere in Judah confirm the annals. The following towns were "utterly destroyed": Beth Shemesh,

16. Ussishkin, *Biblical Lachish*, 219, 302.

Tell Beit Mirsim, Tel 'Eton, Tel Arad, Tel Beer-sheva. In addition, surveys of the Judean Shephelah (lowlands) show a sudden drop in population at this time.[17] Thus the figure from the annals of displacing over two hundred thousand persons is not far-fetched.

The archaeological remains—the prism of Sennacherib, the *bas* relief sculpture, and the excavations of both Lachish and surrounding towns—fill out or supplement our knowledge of the event and help us see the horror that Hezekiah faced at the thought of having Jerusalem conquered by Sennacherib.

Cave of John the Baptist

A New Testament example of archaeology's supplementing texts was discovered by Shimon Gibson.[18] In 1999 Gibson and his team discovered a cave in the hill country of Judea west of Jerusalem (and just west of Ain Karim, John the Baptist's home village, according to Christian tradition), in which ritual activity had been carried out beginning in the Late Hellenistic period. The cave, measuring 24 by 3.5 meters, is situated in the Wadi Esh-Shemmarin, about one kilometer from the ancient village of Suba and about two kilometers from Ain Karim. In the cave are crude drawings, one of a man whom Gibson concluded represents John the Baptist (because the figure resembles John the Baptist as depicted in Byzantine art).[19] Although the cave was in use as early as the Iron age as a water reservoir and later in the Early Hellenistic period as a place of ritual washing, it was sometime in the first century CE that a religious sect took it over and practiced occasional (he suggests yearly) ritual immersions and foot washings. There are a *miqveh* and a place evidently used for foot washings (marked by a carving of a foot on the cave floor) that were used in the first century.[20]

Evidently no one lived in the cave, since there were almost no material remains recovered from the floor except broken pottery. Further, the pottery was mostly one-handled jugs instead of a full range of vessels that one might use in a house. Gibson surmises that the jugs were used in the ritual washings. Then, after the rituals, they evidently smashed the jugs into many pieces. Not a single intact vessel was found, while over one hundred thousand sherds were recovered. The

17. Ussishkin, *Biblical Lachish*, 275.
18. Gibson, *Cave*.
19. Ibid., 4, 11–13.
20. Ibid., 207, 173, 170, 161–62.

sherds date from the late first century BCE to the early second century CE.[21]

Fast-forward from the first century to the Byzantine era when the drawings were etched into the plastered cave walls. There are depicted on the walls, among others, a crude figure of a man, a severed head, and a severed arm. Gibson believes the man to be John the Baptist, the head to represent his beheading, and the arm to point to a relic kept somewhere in the cave (perhaps an arm bone attributed to John the Baptist). He thinks the Byzantine monks gathered there for special worship services in which the leader told the story of John the Baptist by referring to the cave drawings.[22]

But why, asks Gibson, did the Byzantine monks regard the cave as a holy site? Here he looks at some patristic texts and medallions that talk about John the Baptist's association with nearby Ain Karim and about his mother Elizabeth's flight from Herod the Great with the infant John. Gibson opines that Elizabeth hid in the cave to escape Herod's men, later that John as a boy lived in the cave while he tended sheep in this "wilderness" area, and that still later John used the cave as a place of baptism for those hearing his message. This, argues Gibson, is the "wilderness" of Luke 1:80 (and not Qumran as it has become the fashion to conclude). John's association with the cave was remembered and celebrated in the Byzantine era.[23]

Though historians may question some of Gibson's conclusions, one can certainly admire his careful collection of both artifacts and texts. In doing so, he may well have expanded our knowledge of the youthful life of an important New Testament character.

Archaeology Confirms the Historicity of the Bible

On the one hand, scholars seem quick to affirm that archaeology cannot "prove the Bible." Leslie Hoppe, in his brief introduction to biblical archaeology in 1984, noted that "[s]ome people seek to use archaeology as a means to demonstrate the historicity of the Bible." He pronounces "such people" fundamentalist Christians. He allows that efforts to "undergird the historical accuracy of the Bible" are well intentioned but of "limited value."[24] Over thirty years ago, Moyer and Matthews lamented their discovery that most of the Bible handbooks only used

21. Ibid., 155–59.
22. Ibid., 59–67.
23. Ibid., 30–31, 80–83, 213.
24. Hoppe, *Biblical Archaeology*, 5.

archaeology to "prove the accuracy of the Bible . . . and [they feed] off a need to authenticate theological positions. . . ."[25] Milton Moreland cautions that "[u]sing archaeology as a way to 'prove' the veracity of New Testament stories can quickly lead to a 'show-and-tell' approach that values a defense of the literary material over attempts to critically examine the origins of Christianity."[26] One of the great ones in archaeology, Roland de Vaux, insisted that using archaeology as an apologetic attempt to prove the Bible was a "wrong use" of this academic discipline.[27] Likewise James Charlesworth concludes in an essay that "[a]rchaeology is not irrelevant for faith. It is also not essential for it. Yet, while archaeology cannot form faith, it can help inform faith."[28] Shimon Gibson agrees: "As an archaeologist, I am constantly being asked whether the purpose of my work is to seek proof of the stories and events as they appear in the Old and New Testaments. My answer is emphatically that this is not possible. . . ."[29]

So, archaeology is not about "proving" the Bible. Yet archaeologists still do seek to establish the historicity (or nonhistoricity) of certain events and characters of the Bible by using the material remains. For example, Charlesworth himself, even after he eschews using archaeology to establish the historicity of the New Testament, notes in a couple of places that "there is archaeological evidence to support the Gospel record. . . ."[30] Gibson several times in his monograph notes that his archaeological research has established the historicity of the John the Baptist story.[31] Even Dever tries to establish a "historical core" for the Hebrew Bible.[32]

Thus, on the one hand, scholars want to distance themselves from any attempts to "prove" the Bible's historicity using material remains; but, on the other hand, many cannot resist doing so. No doubt, the consensus on avoiding using archaeology in this way is also a reaction to the old Albright school (see chapter 1). Those who want to show a confirmation of a biblical event, text, or person are not trying to prove the Bible in the old sense. They are not saying, for example, that because

25. Moyer and Matthews, "Use and Abuse," 158.
26. Moreland, "New Testament Courses," 136.
27. De Vaux, "Right and Wrong," 67–68.
28. Charlesworth, "Jesus Research," 59. Cf. Charlesworth, "Archaeology," 3: "Archaeology is unfortunately placarded as an aspect of Jewish and Christian apologetics. But biblical archaeologists are not laboring to prove anything."
29. Gibson, *Cave*, 3.
30. Charlesworth, "Jesus Research," 29. See also p. 34 and Charlesworth, "Archaeology," 13.
31. Gibson, *Cave*, 14 and 213. Also, the subtitle of the work explains that it is really about establishing historicity.
32. Dever, *Biblical Writers*, 271–74.

one can illustrate and confirm the invasion of Sennacherib into Judah that all of the religious claims of the Hebrew Bible are valid. But historians and biblical scholars will ask whether there is any evidence for the historicity of these items.

Certainly, there are some interesting historical "convergences" (to use Dever's language). If archaeology sometimes challenges the historicity of the biblical events and persons (see below), it also supports some of them. Let us offer here two cases, one from the Hebrew Bible and one from the New Testament. In these cases the remains—inscriptions mostly but also remains of buildings and even of whole cities as well as some small finds—support many of the details of the biblical text and at least argue for the plausibility of the biblical event or person.

As we will see, however, the "confirmation" of a biblical event, person, or text is seldom straightforward. This is because, first, the remains removed from the soil have no agenda, theological or otherwise. They are just there and they must be interpreted. Second, they are recovered haphazardly, often even accidentally. Excavation directors must decide where to excavate and may miss some important data by a few feet. Further, many times excavations take place when modern construction projects happen upon ruins. Such excavations—called salvage excavations—take place only because the site for a new building or highway accidentally opened an ancient site. Thus, one cannot be sure that one has all or most of the remains that pertain to a biblical event or person. The confirmation, therefore, often leaves questions unanswered and might even surprise us by additional details. Consequently, this category usually overlaps our first category: Archaeology Supplements the Biblical Text.

Shishak of Egypt

In the late tenth century BCE, the Egyptian Pharaoh Shishak I (or Sheshonq or Shoshenq[33]), founder of the twenty-second dynasty (reigned c. 945–924[34]), invaded Palestine and Syria, probably around

---

33. According to Redford, "Shishak," 1221, the name is from the Libyan *shshnk* and appears in Greek as *sesonchis.* Hence the English transliteration as Sheshonq. Others transliterate "Shoshenq." See Rainey and Notley, *Sacred Bridge,* 185.
34. Higginbotham, "Shishak," 241 suggests 945–924 BCE regnal dates. Dever ("Age of Solomon," 239) agrees with these dates. See Gertoux, "Dating Shoshenq's Campaign," for a list of commonly attributed dates for the reign of Shishak. They all are close to these dates. Redford, "Shishak," 1221, suggests 931–910 also as possible regnal dates.

the year 925[35] BCE. The Old Testament books of 1 Kings and 2 Chronicles narrate the invasion:

1 Kings 14	**2 Chronicles 12**
25: And it came to pass in the fifth year of the reign of Rehoboam that Shishak[36] king of Egypt went up against Jerusalem.	2: [same as 1 Kgs 14:25]
	3: [Shishak] came with 1200 chariots and 60,000 horsemen and the people which came with him from Egypt were innumerable: Libyans, Sukkiyim,[37] and Ethiopians. 4: And he captured the fortress cities which belonged to Judah and he came as far as Jerusalem.
	5–8: [the prophet Shema'ya comes]
	9: [same as 1 Kgs 14:26]
26: And he took the treasures of the house of YHWH and the treasures of the house of the king and he took every- thing even all the golden shields which Solomon had made.	

The fifth year of the reign of Rehoboam would be around 925 BCE according to one chronology of the Israelite kings. The invasion of Shishak can be confirmed by two lines of evidence: inscriptional (three inscriptions) and stratigraphic (the destruction levels in several sites in Israel and Jordan). First, let us consider the inscriptions:

1. The extensive list of conquered cities given on the Bubastite Portal in Karnak, Egypt.

---

35. So, the majority of the suggestions listed in Gertoux, "Dating Shoshenq's Campaign." Rainey and Notley, *Sacred Bridge*, 185 maintain that the invasion was in 926/925 BCE. Dever, "Age of Solomon," 239 maintains that the invasion took place sometime between 930 and 925 BCE. Gertoux, however, argues for a date of 972—some twenty-seven years earlier than the traditional dates.
36. So reads the *Qere* of the Masoretic Text of 1 Kings, as does the text of 2 Chronicles (שישק). The *Ketiv* of 1 Kings reads שושק.
37. Rainey and Notley, *Sacred Bridge*, 171, suggest that this place name refers to the oases of Kharga and Dakhla.

2. The Megiddo *stele* celebrating Shishak's victory.
3. The Egyptian amulet found recently in Jordan.

The more important of the three inscriptions—on a gate or portal in Karnak,[38] Egypt—lists over 150[39] towns destroyed by Shishak in his invasion. We will give the names that Rainey and Notley decipher from the list, noting that certain of these identifications have been disputed.[40] Although some historians claim to be able to make only "two dozen" identifications,[41] Rainey and Notley believe they can identify forty-four places on the list:

The Upper Register

Gaza	Gibeon	Tappuah
Gezer	Beth-Horon	Penuel
Rabbah	Kiriath-jearim	Hadashta
Ta'anach	Aijalon	Succoth?
Shunem	Megiddo	Adam
Beth-Shean	Tel 'Ara	Zemaraim
Rehov	Kh. Burin	Migdal
Hopharaim	Jatt	Tirzah?
Adoraim	Kh. Yemma	Gophna
Mahanaim	Socoh	The Valley

The Upper Register of the inscription, then, witnesses to a military invasion against the northern kingdom of Israel, a surprising incursion in light of 1 Kings 11:40. In that text, Jeroboam I, the future king of the northern kingdom, found refuge in Egypt with Pharaoh Shishak I. But then, only a few years later, we find Shishak invading the very king who had previously been given sanctuary.[42]

---

38. For the photographs of the Bubastite Portal section of the temple of Karnak, see Pritchard, *Texts*, I, Photo 94; and No author, "The Bubastite Portal: Reliefs and Inscriptions at Karnack."
39. There seems to be some disagreement on the exact number of towns listed. Redford, "Shishak," 1222 writes that there are 154 towns but the article No author, "Bubastite Portal," affirms that there are 156 towns listed. Rainey and Notley, *Sacred Bridge*, 185 maintain that there are over 100 names. At any rate, many of the sites are illegible due to destruction of parts of the inscription.
40. Rainey and Notley, *Sacred Bridge*, 186–88. As Dever notes ("Age of Solomon," 240), some dispute certain of the identifications on this list, e.g., Gezer. In particular, Clancy ("Shishak/Shoshenq's Travels") disputes the identification of most of these cities. Yet he agrees with the main contours of the common narrative about Shishak's invasion.
41. Wilson, "Shishak."
42. See Rainey and Notley, *Sacred Bridge*, 186–87.

Fig. 2.2 The Bubastite Portal, Karnak, Egypt. Photo in Pritchard, *Pictures*, photograph, .
349. Used with permission of Princeton University Press.

The Lower Register

Kh. Futeis	Tilon
Jehalleleel	Bet Yurahhima
The Negev	Peleth
Eznites	Bet Anat
Shuhah	Yurza
Edomite (?)	Onam
Hanan	Yordan (?)

The Lower Register seems to focus on the Negev.[43] Various scholars have tried to construct a map of the invasion following a route that includes all of the towns on the list, but the maps look like a fairly disorganized mess. Perhaps Shishak I did not actually destroy all of those

43. Ibid., 187.

towns. Or perhaps the list was never intended to give us a straightforward itinerary of his invasion.[44] At any rate, the details of the list led Rainey and Notley to conclude: "This inscription can only be based on intelligence information gathered during a real campaign by Pharaoh Shoshenq."[45] Thus, they take it as a real itinerary in the main.

Surprisingly, missing from this list is any reference to Jerusalem or to the fortified towns in the Judean highlands. One could get the impression from the biblical narrative that the main thrust of Shishak's campaign was against Judah and especially Jerusalem. But this list gives quite a different impression. According to the list, Shishak attacked widely, especially in the Negev, the Shephelah, and in the northern kingdom of Israel.[46] It is possible, as many have suggested, that the numerous place names on the inscription, many of which have been destroyed over time, were identifying locations in Judea. But what we have does not refer to Judea. So, the list in a sense confirms the biblical text and in a sense it does not.

In addition to the extensive list of towns on the temple in Karnak, there are two smaller inscriptions that have come to light that refer to Shishak. The first of these is an inscription (now fragmentary) made on a *stele* and erected near Megiddo that celebrates Shishak's victories.[47] Inscribed on the fifteen-inch fragment are the words, "Amun's beloved, Shoshenq."[48] Kitchen maintains that the fragment dates to around 925 BCE.[49]

More recently, an Egyptian scarab amulet was found near an ancient copper mine fifty kilometers south of the Dead Sea and twenty-five kilometers northwest of Petra. The scarab had the throne name of Shishak I on it.[50] Taken together, these three inscriptions certainly confirm that there was a Pharaoh named Shishak and that he invaded Palestine about the time he was alleged to have done so.

But the second line of evidence is also interesting. Several towns show a destruction layer that dates approximately to the time of the invasion (c. 925 BCE). The following list of such towns is taken from Dever and A. Mazar.[51] Some of these towns (with asterisks) are also on the Shishak list at Karnak (see above).

44. See Rainey and Notley, *Sacred Bridge*, 185.
45. Ibid.
46. Higginbotham, "Shishak," 242.
47. See e.g., Higginbotham, "Shishak," 242.
48. Kitchen, "Shishak's Military Campaign," 33.
49. Ibid.
50. See Levy, Münger, and Najjar, "Newly Discovered Scarab"; and Gannon, ed., "Amulet."
51. Dever, *Biblical Writers*, 135; Mazar, *Archaeology*, 398, 444; and idem., "1997–1998 Excavations."

Hazor (stratum IX)	Tel Qasile (stratum VIII)
Tel Abu Hawam (stratum III)	*Gezer (stratum VIII)
Tel Keisan (stratum VIII-A)	Tel Batash/Timnah (stratum IV)
*Megiddo (stratum V-a/IV-B)	Tel el-Hama
*Ta'anach (stratum II-B)	Tel es-Saidiyeh (stratum XI)
*Beth Shan (upper stratum V)	Tel el-Mazar
*Tel Rehov	*Arad (stratum XI)
Tel Mevorach (stratum VII)	Beer-sheba
Tel Michal	Kadesh Barnea
Dor[52]	

Thus one can see that the Shishak invasion, referred to in 1 Kings and repeated in 2 Chronicles, was a bigger incursion than it might appear from the biblical text. On the one hand, the long inscription at the Bubastite gate at Karnak, the brief, fragmentary inscription on the *stele* found at Megiddo, and the scarab confirm that there was a Pharaoh named Shishak (or Sheshonq, or Shoshenq). On the other hand, the inscriptional evidence and the stratigraphic evidence of so many towns being destroyed at this time expand our understanding of the invasion. The list from Karnak surprises us at the widespread terror that Shishak I inflicted on the inhabitants of Israel in the late tenth century BCE. But even that list, apparently, is not the full picture since there are several other towns that were destroyed at the same time that are not on the list. Not even the boastful list from Karnak captures all of the brutality. One thing seems clear: Shishak's invasion was a widely experienced, horrible, scorched-earth event. There is no outside confirmation that Shishak came to Jerusalem and carried off the golden shields as the biblical story tells it. But perhaps the inscription makes no mention of Shishak's destroying Jerusalem because he did not do so since Rehoboam bought him off.

Acts 19

Fast-forward nine hundred years to the first century and the spread of early Christianity into the Greco-Roman world.[53] The New Testament

---

52. According to Gertoux, "Dating Sheshonq I's Campaign."
53. For the following cf. Fiensy, "Roman Empire," 42–43.

book of Acts narrates three "missionary journeys" of the apostle Paul. As part of the third missionary tour, Paul is reported to have spent an extended amount of time in the city of Ephesus (Acts 19:10; 20:31). There, he taught in the Jewish synagogue for a while, encountered some Jewish exorcists, and witnessed an anti-Christian, pagan riot.

Although the material remains confirm that Jews had a presence in Ephesus, they do not provide many details. To date, only three inscriptions referring to Jews in Ephesus and some objects with Jewish symbols have been found.[54] The synagogue so far has eluded discovery.

Fig. 2.3 Façade of the Library of Celsus, Ephesus. The "auditorium" was adjacent to it, but the library is a second-century CE structure. See Erdemgil et al., *Ephesus*, 41, who dates the library to 117 CE. Photograph by the author.

Luke then says that Paul removed himself from the synagogue to teach in the lecture hall (σχολη) of Tyrannus (Acts 19:9). A person named Tyrannus has been attested in an inscription, but we cannot be certain that this is the same one as in Acts. Additionally, an inscription referring to an αυδειτωριον (*audeitorion*) or "auditorium" has been found. This was a lecture hall adjacent to the library.[55] The identification with

54. G. H. R. Horsley, "Inscriptions of Ephesus," 122–25. The objects are four oil lamps with menorahs; a piece of glass with a menorah, an *ethrog*, a *lulab*, and a shofar painted on it; a menorah carved on a step in front of the library; and a gem with a scriptural reference. See also Yamauchi, *New Testament Cities*, 110.

55. Hemer, *Acts*, 120–21. See also Yamauchi, *New Testament Cities*, 100.

the Tyrannus of Acts and with his lecture hall is not certain but is certainly plausible.

The riot (Acts 19:23–40) has attracted attention due to the numerous epigraphical and classical parallels to the text of Acts. The details of this section lead to the conclusion that the author at least knew the culture of Ephesus and may have been present at the riot.[56] The reference to Ephesus as a νεωχορος (neokoros) or "temple warden" city (Acts 19:35); the mention of the clerk or scribe as the leader of the people (γραμματευς, grammateus; Acts 19:35); the several reminders that Artemis was acclaimed as "great" by the Ephesians (Acts 19:27, 28, 34, 35); the statement that Artemis was honored in many other places (Acts 19:27); the reference to silversmiths (αργυροκοπος, argyrokopos; Acts 19:24); and calling the regular assembly of Ephesus the εννομος εκκλησια (ennomos ekklesia, Acts 19:39)—are all attested word for word in the inscriptions from Ephesus.[57]

One inscription alone can illustrate the wealth of finds that appear to confirm the text of Acts 19:

> Good Fortune! The *silversmiths* of the first and greatest metropolis of Asia, the thrice-honored *temple guardian* (*NEOKOROS*) of the venerable Ephesians erected [this monument to] Valerius Festus, the flower of his ancestors, creator of many works in both Asia and Ephesus, according to the heroic Antonines, who improved the harbor [of the Artemisium]. [Festus] has made himself savior and in all things a benefactor.[58]

The words in italics are two of the terms given in Acts 19. Edwards dates the inscription (because of the reference to the Antonine emperors) to the late second or early third century CE. The inscription indicates that the guild of silversmiths referred to in Acts was still in existence and still supporting the sacred temples of Ephesus.

Although no silver shrines have yet been found like those named in Acts 19:24, the oft-cited Salutaris inscription from Ephesus describes a golden statuette of Artemis. In addition, terra-cotta figurines of Artemis standing in a niche have been found that roughly correspond to that indicated in Acts.[59] Further, the zeal with which the Ephesians

---

56. Koester, "Ephesos," 119–40. Koester notes that the details demonstrate the author's knowledge of Ephesian religious and political life but affirms that these details do not prove that the story is historical.

57. See Koester, "Ephesos," 130; Hemer, *Book of Acts*, 121–23; Richard Oster, "Historical Commentary," 112–15; Trebilco, "Asia," 291–362, esp. 318–56; Gasque, "Historical Value," 186; Edwards, "Archaeology."

58. Translated by Edwards, "Archaeology," 26–27. The italics are mine.

defended the cult of Artemis in the riot described in Acts 19 is well known from an inscription. According to this text, they sentenced forty-five persons to death for mistreating sacred items from Artemis.[60] More generally, historians have noted the frequent attestation of labor guilds, such as the silversmiths' guild to which Demetrius belonged (Acts 19:24–27). The inscriptions from Asia refer to guilds of all kinds, including silversmiths. Further, other incidents of rioting at the instigation of these labor unions are indicated in the inscriptions.[61] The gathering of labor unions, it seems, often could result in outbreaks of unrest in the cities of Asia Minor. Thus, the story of the riot in Ephesus narrated in Acts 19 is plausible. There is a striking number of details attested from inscriptions.

Fig. 2.4 Theater of Ephesus where the riot of Acts 19 took place. Photograph by the author.

59. Oster, "Historical Commentary," 71–73; Hemer, *Book of Acts*, 121; Trebilco, "Asia," 336, 356; and Mussies, "Pagans," 189. The Salutaris inscription was published with translation by J. H. Oliver, *Sacred Gerusia*.
60. Oster, "Historical Commentary," 97–98; Trebilco, "Asia," 331.
61. Trebilco, "Asia," 336, 338; Oster, "Historical Commentary," 75–77.

Taken together, these numerous inscriptions and other material remains offer quite a bit of evidence supporting the general narrative of the New Testament book of Acts chapter 19, Paul's experiences in the city of Ephesus. They do not prove that the events narrated really happened, but they do demonstrate that the author (or his source) knew the culture and customs of the Ephesians and probably had spent time there. In this way, the archaeology of Ephesus "confirms" the biblical text or, actually, makes the narrative of Acts 19 plausible.[62]

Thus our two examples of archaeology confirming a biblical text only do so in a rather vague and general way. It appears that this is true for most, if not all, of the genuine "confirmations" of the Bible through archaeology. As the great archaeologist Roland de Vaux wrote in his seminal essay of 1970, "the 'confirmation' brought by archaeology to the biblical narrative is rarely without ambiguity."[63] Such confirmations then do not prove the Bible but they do help one distinguish between a historically based narrative and a narrative more legendary.

Archaeology Contradicts the Bible

Not all archaeological finds confirm the biblical stories. Sometimes the remains seem to tell a different tale than the Bible's version. When that happens scholars react in different ways. Yet, just as archaeology's "confirmation" of the Bible is seldom straightforward (see above), so the contradiction is also seldom a "no-brainer."

The Exodus

One of the narratives that still raise controversy is the Hebrew Bible's account of the exodus. The traditional date of the exodus—based on presumed literal chronological references in 1 Kings 6:1 and Judges 11:27—is the mid-fifteenth century BCE. But recently, a "consensus" date of mid-thirteenth century BCE has developed.[64] In the early days of using archaeology to interpret the Bible, scholars such as William F. Albright and his students believed that their excavations were confirming a thirteenth-century BCE exodus just as the Old Testament

---

62. Cf. Edwards, "Archaeology," 62: "Some 18 historical references or terms occur in Acts 19:23-40. Apart from the personal identities of Demetrius and Alexander, all these references and terms are repeated and reported in the archaeological or inscriptional remains of Ephesus. . . ."
63. De Vaux, "Right and Wrong," 77.
64. For the traditional and consensus dates, see Hoffmeier, *Israel*, 124–25; and Geraty, "Exodus Dates," 56–59.

seems to indicate.[65] They believed that their finds at the ancient sites of Debir, Bethel, and Hazor proved that the conquest of Canaan (which according to the Bible happened forty years after the exodus) had taken place just as the book of Joshua reported it.[66] Then the edifice began to crumble.

Perhaps the most cogent refutation of a thirteenth-century exodus has been done by Israel Finkelstein and Neil Asher Silberman.[67] They employ basically three lines of argument: 1) There is direct historical reference in Egyptian records neither to Israel's sojourn in nor to its departure from Egypt. 2) The conditions at that time would have made an unwanted departure of such a large group from Egypt nearly impossible. 3) The subsequent "conquest" (forty years later) of Canaan is not attested archaeologically. Their expanded case for abandoning the exodus story as it exists in the Hebrew Bible is as follows:

The story of Israel in Egypt looks like a vague memory of the Hyksos infiltration, hegemony, and subsequent expulsion from Egypt.[68] The Hyksos were West Asiatic, Semitic immigrants who entered Egypt gradually and peacefully but eventually established the fifteenth Dynasty (1670–1570 BCE). Their expulsion in 1570 BCE sounds to Finkelstein and Silberman like the exodus story.

There is no reference in Egyptian literature or in the inscriptions of Israelites passing through the border from Egypt to Canaan. The border of Egypt was carefully controlled. A group passing through it at this time should have left a record.[69] Further, any group escaping from the Nile Delta at this time against the will of the pharaoh could easily have been stopped by a series of Egyptian forts in the Sinai and Canaan.[70]

There is no archaeological trace of Israel in the Sinai Peninsula from this time. A large group camping for forty years—especially at Kadesh Barnea (Num 33:37–38; Deut 1:46; 2:14) and Ezion Geber (Num 33:35, 36)—should have left something behind.[71] Nor is there archaeological evidence for the existence of the people groups of Edom, Moab, and Ammon in the thirteenth century. Further, the following cities which figure prominently in the conquest narratives did not exist (i.e., were

---

65. Hoffmeier, *Israel*, 3–4.
66. Finkelstein and Silberman, *Bible Unearthed*, 79–80.
67. Ibid.
68. Ibid., 53.
69. Ibid., 59.
70. Ibid., 61.
71. Ibid., 63.

not occupied significantly) in the Late Bronze Age (thirteenth century BCE): Jericho, Ai, Gibeon, Arad, and Heshbon.[72]

Fig. 2.5 Neolithic tower, Jericho. The city in the LB age had "scanty" remains. Photograph by the author.

Finally, the geographical details, while they do not fit with the thirteenth century BCE, do fit well with the situation in the seventh century BCE. It looks like the author(s) imposed geography from their day onto an old story. Finkelstein and Silberman conclude that the exodus story is a combination of the memory of the Hyksos expulsion and contemporary (i.e. seventh century) geographical details.[73]

The response to such arguments has been varied. Some now take it for granted that the exodus narrative is legendary and unhistorical.[74] But others want to find some basis for a thirteenth-century BCE exodus and conquest.[75] Kitchen, for example, who gives a thoughtful and nuanced defense of the historicity of the exodus, though admitting that there are "negatives" in the evidence, maintains that the argu-

---

72. Ibid., 64, 82. For Jericho, see also the recent analysis of Nigro, "Tell es-Sultan." Nigro writes that the city was occupied in the LB age but that the remains are "scanty" (16).

73. Finkelstein and Silberman, *Bible Unearthed*, 69.

74. So Dever, *Biblical Writers*, "[T]he overwhelming archaeological evidence today of largely indigenous origins for early Israel leaves no room for an exodus from Egypt or a 40-year pilgrimage through the Sinai wilderness" (99). See also Hawkins's (*Israel*, 100) summary of the scholarly consensus about Jericho: "The current consensus of archaeologists and biblical scholars is that the results of the excavations at Tell es-Sultan contradict the account of the conquest of Jericho as presented in the book of Joshua."

75. See Kitchen, *Reliability*, 311–12.

ments he has compiled do "favor acceptance of [the exodus] having had a definite historical basis."[76] Hoffmeier[77] offers evidence similar to Kitchen. He argues for plausibility of an exodus based on the fact that Semites were known to live in Egypt for several centuries before and after the alleged Hebrew exodus.[78] Hawkins argues for a "scaled down" conquest in which the towns of Jericho and Ai were occupied in the Late Bronze Age but had only meager settlements. Thus, in this view, Israel did conquer these towns but the towns were not as large and powerful as we have previously understood them to have been.[79]

Still others want to suggest a date other than the "consensus" date of the thirteenth century BCE (or the traditional date of mid-fifteenth century BCE for that matter).[80] Many of those arguing especially for a date earlier than the traditional date want to associate the Hebrew exodus with the violent, volcanic eruption of the island of Thera (modern Santorini) in the Aegean, which sent a tsunami east and south and destroyed many towns along the coast.[81] Complicating this effort, however, is the fact that the date of this eruption itself is also disputed.[82]

Finally, in reference to the conquest cities, some want to suggest that the sites commonly identified as the alleged Canaanite cities are not the correct locations. As we indicated above, many of the cities allegedly destroyed by Joshua were evidently not even occupied in the Late Bronze Age (Jericho, Ai, Gibeon, Arad, and Heshbon). For example, the site called by the Arabs et-Tell is usually taken to be the original location for the Canaanite city of Ai, which was according to the book of Joshua destroyed by the Israelites (Joshua 8). But the problem, as Finkelstein and Silberman pointed out, is that there was no occupation of et-Tell in the Late Bronze Age. Thus, the story in Joshua does not have archaeological confirmation. But now, a new excavation at Khir-

---

76. Ibid., 312. Kitchen does grant that the lack of Egyptian records mentioning Israelites working in the Delta and the lack of archaeological remains in the Sinai are "negatives," but he also lists several "positives."

77. Hoffmeier, *Israel*. He wants to give "indirect evidence" for an exodus to show plausibility (226).

78. Cf. Bietak, "Exodus Evidence," 36 who grants that his evidence (similar to Kitchen and Hoffmeier) is "symptomatic," i.e., "an incident recorded and preserved in an Egyptian text by accident that doubtless occurred repeatedly."

79. Hawkins, *Israel*, 105, 111.

80. For a list of suggested dates, see Geraty, "Exodus Dates," 60.

81. See these views explained in Higham, "Radiocarbon Dating," 86; Harris, "Thera Theories," 97–100; Wiener, "Dating the Theran Eruption"; and Schulze et al., "The WAVE." This 2015 collection of articles from a wide range of perspectives and views on the exodus shows that the conviction that there was a literal Hebrew exodus from Egypt is not dead.

82. See ibid. Archaeologists (using standard methods of archaeological dating) and scientists (using carbon fourteen dating) place the eruption somewhere between the seventeenth and sixteenth centuries BCE.

bet el Maqatir, one kilometer away from et-Tell, which was occupied in the Late Bronze Age, is being suggested by some as the actual site of the biblical Ai.[83] This thesis is a possibility, but whether one can find such a solution for all of the cities listed above that were allegedly destroyed by the Israelites but for which no archaeological evidence for occupation is present is another question.

Whatever the response, it appears that the exodus story is one of those that archaeological remains do not confirm and probably actually contradict, especially if one insists on a thirteenth-century BCE exodus. But the caveat is that much of the argument above is from silence.[84] As James Hoffmeier observes, so far no papyri from the Nile Delta (where the Bible locates the Israelites) have been found. To expect documents confirming that the Israelites were there may be expecting too much.[85] Thus, as in the previous section ("Archaeology Confirms the Historicity of the Bible"), so here. The "contradiction" is not straightforward; it is not, in my judgment, a sure thing that there was no exodus event at all. There is no denying that archaeology has made acceptance of the exodus problematic, but the nature of the incomplete archaeological remains cautions us against a definitive conclusion. One conclusion seems safe, based on the recent appearance of the collection of essays edited by Levy, Schneider, and Propp:[86] the exodus continues to fascinate biblical scholars and scientists alike.

Roman Soldiers in Capernaum?

A story of a "centurion's" slave (or boy or son) is given in the Q source of Matthew (8:5–13) and Luke (7:1–10), with a story only very slightly different in detail in the Gospel of John (4:46–54). The story is about a man of prominence (a centurion in Matthew and Luke; a "royal [official]" in John) whose slave (Luke), boy (Matthew), or son (John) is extremely ill. The man goes to see Jesus (or sends Jewish elders to Jesus in Luke's version) to ask him to heal the slave/boy/son. The elders plead his case before Jesus (in Luke's version) by informing Jesus that

---

83. See Govier, "Top Ten Discoveries"; Wood, "Excavations."
84. Cf. Dever, *Recent Archaeological*, 24 on the Patriarchs and archaeology: "The point is not that archaeology has disproved the historicity of the Patriarchs, but simply that it has not gotten beyond the literary tradition that we had all along in the Hebrew Bible."
85. Hoffmeier, "Out of Egypt," 4–5. As a matter of fact, as Kitchen observes, 99 percent of all the papyri at any location in Egypt have been lost (*Reliability*, 311).
86. Levy, Schneider, and Propp, *Israel's Exodus.*

the prominent man has paid for the local synagogue to be built.[87] We may summarize the three narratives as follows:

Matthew 8:5–13	Luke 7:1–10	John 4:46–54[88]
5: The **CENTURION** has a "boy" who is horribly tormented with an illness	2: The **CENTURION'S** "slave" is ill to the point of death	46: A *ROYAL (official)* has a "son" who is ill
		47: The son will soon die
7: Jesus volunteers to go heal him	3: He sends the elders of the Jews to implore Jesus to heal him	49: The *ROYAL (official)* begs Jesus to come to his house before his "little child" dies
	4–5: The elders say the centurion loves "our nation" and has built the local synagogue	
8: The **CENTURION** says Jesus need only say the word from a distance and the healing will happen	6–7: While Jesus is still far away, the **CENTURION** sends word that Jesus only need say the word from afar and the "boy" can be healed	
9: He has **soldiers** under his authority	8: He has **soldiers** under his authority	
		51: His "boy" is healed
		53: He recalls the hour Jesus had said your "son" will live

The historical problem with this story is that it is very unlikely that a Roman centurion (a Roman officer with a company of sixty to a hundred soldiers[89]) lived in Capernaum (which would suppose a garrison of Roman troops stationed there). Jesus was there during the rule of Antipas (governed 4 BCE–39 CE), during which time there were no Roman troops stationed in Galilee. Antipas's government was semi-independent and ran its own security.[90] Therefore, it is *prima facie* unlikely that there were Roman soldiers stationed there. No other doc-

87. See Corbo, "Capernaum," I.868.
88. See Brown, *John*, I.192–93 for the argument that the story in John's Gospel is a variant of the story in Matt/Luke.
89. See Parker, "Manipulus"; Parker and Watson, "Cohors," and "Centurio." There were thirty maniples in a legion, each with from 120 to 200 men. Each maniple had two centuries commanded each by a centurion.
90. See Sherwin-White, *Roman Society*, 123–24; Reed, *Archaeology*, 162. Schürer, Vermes, and Miller,

47

ument or text mentions Roman soldiers being garrisoned anywhere in Galilee during this time, certainly not in Capernaum.[91]

Further, there is no archaeological support for a Roman garrison there in the first century CE. After excavating in Capernaum—on both the Franciscan side and the Greek Orthodox side—no evidence for such a garrison has been found. There is no ruin of an army barrack, no *palaestra*, and no theater. The closest one might come to any archaeological support for a Roman military presence is the second or third century CE bath in the Greek Orthodox sector.[92] Since the floor plan is similar to a bath found in En-Gedi—dating to the first century CE and used there by a Roman garrison—some maintain that this bath in Capernaum was probably also a Roman bath and thus that it attests to the presence of Roman soldiers in the village in the second or third century. One archaeologist also suggests that under the floor of the second/third-century bath *might* be a first-century Roman bath's ruins.[93] We cannot, however, deal with speculations but with *realia*. The fact is there is no evidence for a first-century bath. But even if one could prove that there was a first-century CE bath, it still might not prove that there was a Roman garrison there. One scholar doubts that this was a Roman bath at all. Jews also visited baths and there are numerous references to their existence in villages. Thus, the bath might not attest to a Roman military presence in Capernaum at any period.[94]

Some New Testament scholars maintain that Antipas's soldiers were gentiles and were "organized on Roman lines" and, therefore, their leader was given a Roman title. We do read that Antipas's father, Herod the Great, had soldiers from non-Jewish nations (Thracians, Germans, and Gauls; Josephus, *Ant.* 17–198).[95] But the problem becomes one of plausibility. We have a story about a non-Jew with the title "centurion." That certainly looks like this person is alleged to have been a

History, I.455–70 state that after 44 CE Galilee was under Roman authority. Freyne, *Galilee*, 73 wrote that after the death of Agrippa I, Galilee had "its first immediate contact with direct Roman rule."

91. Bultmann, *History*, 38–39, concluded that this pericope was a variant of the "Syro-Phoenician Woman," story (Mark 7:24–31 and par.) and that the scenes of both stories "are imaginary."

92. Reed, *Archaeology*, 155; Crossan and Reed, *Excavating*, 88; Matillah, "Capernaum," 227; Laughlin, "Capernaum," 56. Reed finds archaeological support for a Roman military presence in the second century CE from an inscription indicating that Roman soldiers built for Emperor Hadrian a road near Capernaum (Reed, *Archaeology*, 156). For the location of the baths see the town plan in Matillah, "Capernaum," 219.

93. Laughlin, "Capernaum," 57.

94. Matillah, "Capernaum," 227. She cites m. Abod. Zar. 3:4, a story about Rabbi Gamaliel using a bath house in Acco.

95. Marshall, *Luke*, 279; Bond, "Roman Centurion"; Bovon, *Luke 1*, 260; Nolland, *Matthew*, 354.

Roman military officer and that there was, therefore, a garrison of Roman soldiers stationed in Capernaum in the first half of the first century CE.

So there is no archaeological support for a Roman garrison—and, therefore, no archaeological support for a centurion—in Capernaum during the time of Jesus. There are only the remains of a bath, but the bath did not exist, according to the evidence we have now, in the first century CE. The bath may not even have been a Roman bath in the first place. There is no archaeological support for Luke's and Matthew's reading that the prominent man in the story was a Roman centurion. But the question the historian now must ask is: Does the lack of archaeological evidence prove there were no Roman soldiers there? Again, the "contradiction" to the text is not straightforward but is based on silence. The historian must decide if the silence is adequate to dispute the narrative.

Archaeology Clarifies a Biblical Text

Direct Clarification

We will divide this section into two subsections, as indicated above. We will consider ways archaeology clarifies a text either by directly explaining a reference or verse or indirectly by helping us to imagine the background to the text. The most obvious way archaeological remains clarify a text directly is by offering an illustration of an object. Strange, in his essay cited in chapter 1,[96] suggests a lamp as an example of this form of clarification. I want to present here two quite different illustrations: The first is actually a person; the second is a much larger example, a large farm or estate in Palestine in the late Second Temple period.

1. Jehu (Ninth Century BCE)

One of the simplest ways for archaeology to clarify a biblical text is to illustrate an object. But let us first of all illustrate a person: Jehu, king of the northern state of Israel from around 845 to 818 BCE.[97] His reign is narrated in 1 Kings chapters 9–10 and in summary fashion in 2 Chronicles 22:7–9. He is referred to again in 1 Kings 19:16–17 and in

96. Strange, "Sayings of Jesus."
97. Or 841–814 or 842–815 BCE. See Thiel, "Jehu," for the various dates.

Hosea 1:4. His reign was evaluated positively by the Deuteronomistic historian, but not so positively by the prophet Hosea. Be that as it may, Jehu has the distinction of being the only Israelite monarch ever represented in art and one of the first Israelites of any sort to be depicted. The Black Obelisk of Shalmaneser III (reigned 858–824 BCE) stands a little over two meters high. It is composed of black limestone and is inscribed with twenty panels of text and pictures. The obelisk depicts Shalmaneser's conquests over the west (i.e., the area west of Assyria). One of those depicted in a prostrate position before the king is labeled "Jehu, son of Omri." The depiction of Jehu appears stylized; he looks almost exactly like the thirteen Israelite gift bearers who follow him. Yet, whether this is an accurate portrait of Jehu,[98] it still gives us a fairly good look at the way Israelites dressed and groomed in the ninth century BCE. "Jehu" of the Black Obelisk gives us an image to think about when we read his name in the Bible.

Fig. 2.6 Jehu prostrated before Shalmaneser III; from Black Obelisk of Shalmaneser. Photograph in Pritchard, *Pictures*, photograph 351. Used with permission of Princeton University Press.

2. Ramat ha-Nadiv (First Century CE)

Fast-forward eight hundred years to the area just northeast of Caesarea Maritima. Since the publication of Johannes Herz's "Large Estates in

98. Amerding, "Shalmaneser," 409, concludes that it is not an accurate portrait of the king. For photographs of the obelisk see King and Stager, *Life*, 261 and 262 and Pritchard, *Ancient Near East*, photograph 100a.

Palestine at the Time of Jesus" in 1928, it has been assumed that Jesus's parables were alluding to real economic conditions in Lower Galilee.[99] Whether historians have accepted that all, or even most, of these parables originated from the historical Jesus, they nonetheless have seen in the parables genuine reflections of economic life in Palestine/Israel. Specifically, several of Jesus's parables assume that there were large agricultural estates in ancient Palestine/Israel. Certainly these estates were not as large as the celebrated ones we read about that were found elsewhere in the Roman Empire, but they were large enough to require tenant farmers, agricultural slaves, and bailiffs to care for the landowner's farm. Luke 16:1–7 speaks of debts of 100 measures of oil and 100 measures of wheat, which would have required at least a medium-sized estate to produce. Herz maintained that one would have needed 160 olive trees and forty acres of wheat to lend such a sum.

Fig. 2.7 Artist's reconstruction by Balage Balough of the mansion at Ramat ha-Nadiv (reconstruction by Balage Balough and first used in Hirschfeld and Feinberg-Vamosh, "Country Gentleman's Estate," 18–19). On the upper right is the mansion. On the lower left are the swimming pool and bath house. Used by permission.

The same sort of conclusion can be drawn from the Parable of the Talents (Matt 25:14–30 // Luke 19:11–27), the Parable of the Debtors (Luke 7:41–43 // Matt 18:24–34), and the Parable of the Unforgiving

99. Herz, "Grossgrundbesitz."

Servant (Matt 18:21–35). These parables speak of large sums of money that imply great wealth, and great wealth usually implies large estates. Still other parables depict scenes on a large estate. The Parable of the Rich Fool (Luke 12:16–21), for instance, describes an estate owner hoarding grain in a manner reminiscent of an account in Josephus (*Vita* 119) about the granary of Queen Berenice. Luke 17:7 refers to a man's servant plowing his field for him. Matthew 20:1–15 describes a large landowner who has so much land he needed to hire day laborers to work it.[100] But what did these large estates look like? How did the landowners live and how did the laborers live? We now have an excellent example of a large estate that was found just northeast of Caesarea Maritima on the Ramat ha-Nadiv ridge.

Fig. 2.8 Swimming Pool of "The Mansion," Ramat ha-Nadiv. Photograph by the author.

The estate on the Ramat ha-Nadiv ridge controlled 2,500 acres, according to Yizhar Hirschfeld, the excavator of this ruin. On the estate was a complex of buildings, one of which, the "Mansion," had 150 rooms and was decorated in elaborate marble panels. There was a multistoried tower standing guard over the mansion and nearby was the owner's

---

100. Ibid.

swimming pool and bathhouse. The estate owner had all of the ameni- ties that his age could provide. This mansion was the "Downton Abbey" of its day. This was clearly the estate of a very wealthy person.

On the other side of the ridge there was another ruin connected to the first one by an ancient road. This enclosed area contained a thresh- ing floor, oil press, and wine presses (along with a *miqveh*). This was a more modest construction that Hirschfeld concluded was the agri- cultural center of the estate. Unlike other large estates in the ancient empire (even in Palestine), there was no village associated with it. The agricultural workers must have lived in the complex, perhaps as slaves, or traveled there each day to work as day laborers.[101] Looking at these ruins with one eye and at the Gospels' parables with the other, one can quickly imagine how the estates functioned and how the parables are attempting to tell the story. This estate illustrates the typical large estate so often featured in the parables attributed to Jesus.[102]

Indirect Clarification

In this subcategory we will present examples of archaeology's clarify- ing the Bible by providing background and context for the biblical text or story. Most of archaeology's contribution to biblical study is of this sort. The number of specific verses explained by an archaeological find or of narratives clarified by a find is small. Mostly archaeology helps the biblical interpreter to imagine the story. We will consider below: morbidity, religion, and economy.

1. Morbidity (Iron Age to Crusader Period Israel)

The reader often assumes that when Isaiah wrote his fabulous poetry, he was reasonably comfortable. We just presume that, aside from occa- sional illnesses, most persons in antiquity were fairly healthy, even as they are in western societies today. One way to test this assumption that archaeologists have developed is the examination of ancient fecal remains.[103] When investigated, the fecal remains of three latrines from three different eras and locations (Iron II period Jerusalem; Early

---

101. See Hirschfeld, "Bath and Fortress"; Hirschfeld, *Ramat Hanadiv*; and Hirschfeld and Vamosh, "Country Gentleman's Estate."
102. For further information, see Fiensy, *Social History*, 21–73; and Fiensy, *Christian Origins*, 98–117.
103. Harter, Bouchet, Mumcuoglu, and Zias, "Toilet Practices"; Mitchell and Tepper, "Intestinal Para- sitic Worm Eggs"; Edward Neufeld, "Hygiene Conditions"; Zias, "Death and Disease"; Cahill et al., "It Had to Happen"; Reinhard and Araújo, "Archaeoparasitology."

Roman Qumran; and Crusader Acco) yielded about the same results. The remains of all three latrines were full of intestinal parasites, whipworms mostly but also tapeworms and roundworms. In the Iron Age Jerusalem sample, each milliliter of organic residue had about 11,000 parasite eggs in it. Eighty-five percent of the eggs were whipworm and 15 percent were tapeworm. At the Qumran latrine, archaeologists found evidence of whipworm, tapeworm, and roundworm. The results from Acco were similar (whipworm and tapeworm). The parasites were ingested, for the most part, as a result of either undercooked meat or as the result of handling, and subsequently ingesting, fecal remains (e.g., on vegetables).[104] The presence of parasite eggs in the fecal remains of humans indicates a very poor hygienic environment as well as undercooked meat and population crowding.[105]

"Parasites are the major cause of ill health and early death in the world today."[106] The parasites were/are not in themselves usually fatal, but the problem was that they competed with the "host" for food. They might in times of plenty only cause a mild anemia. But if a person's diet was challenged, the parasites could hasten starvation. Children would be especially vulnerable because their growth would be stunted due to "vitamin deficiencies and impaired growth."[107] Mitchell and Tepper observe grimly, "Those with the most parasites in their intestines . . . die from starvation first."[108]

But there can also be more readily lethal consequences of intestinal parasites. Extreme cases could even lead to diarrhea, bowl blockages, malabsorption of food, and hence to death.[109] Given the apparent prevalence of the parasites, those biblical characters might not have felt so well after all. Some individuals (most?) went through life never knowing what it felt like to be healthy.[110]

2a. Religion (Iron Age Israel)

King Hezekiah can say in prayer, "O, YHWH of hosts, you are the God of Israel who sits on the cherubim. *You are God alone*" (Isa 37:16). This

---

104. Harter et al., "Toilet Practices," surmise that the residents of Qumran also contracted the parasites by ritually bathing after an infected person (582).
105. Reinhard and Araújo, "Archaeoparasitology," 498.
106. Ibid., 495.
107. Mitchell and Tepper, "Intestinal Parasitic Worm Eggs," 93–94.
108. Ibid., 94.
109. Ibid.
110. For more information on the parasites and other chronic and widespread illnesses, see Reed, "Instability"; King and Stager, *Life*, 71–75; and Zias, "Death and Disease."

is a perfect monotheistic confession. But how did the common folk feel about it? It is almost a truism of history that the ordinary person was rarely "orthodox."[111] Theological orthodoxy was a luxury for the religious elite, and archaeology is now bearing this out as two finds indicate. The Old Testament makes at least forty references to "Asherah."[112] Sometimes these references seem to describe a wooden pole or tree; at other times they are imagining a goddess.[113] But, in reality, it is not surprising when archaeologists occasionally find images of a fertility goddess and presume it to be Asherah. What is surprising, however, is finding evidence that some Israelites worshiped Asherah as the consort of Yahweh. Most notable is the excavation of Kuntillet 'Ajrûd in the Sinai Peninsula. The site, excavated in 1978, dates from the Iron II period. Among the finds were two large pithos jars that had Hebrew inscriptions and drawings. The inscriptions were made in four media: incised on stone, incised on pottery, ink on pottery, and ink on plaster.[114] Four of the inscriptions refer to YHWH and his Asherah:

- "I have [b]lessed you to YHWH of Shômrôn (Samaria) and to his *asherah*." (ink on pottery; Pithos A)

- "I have blessed you by YHWH of Têmān and His *asherah*." (ink on pottery; Pithos B)

- "to YHWH of the Têmān and His *asherah*." (ink on pottery; Pithos B)

- "[May] He lengthen their days and may they be sated [. . .] recount to [Y]HWH of Têmān and His *asherah*."[115] (ink on wall plaster)

Is the *asherah* of these four inscriptions the Canaanite fertility goddess, or does the word mean Yahweh's sacred pole? If the former, then these people believed that Yahweh had a consort. As Ze'ev Meshel notes, the religious reforms of Hezekiah and Josiah apparently did not reach 'Ajrûd.[116]

Item two is a terra-cotta cult stand found in the city of Ta'anach in

111. Fiensy, *Social History*, 2; Dever, *Did God Have a Wife?*, 314–15. See also the interesting essay by Neusner, "Babylonian Jewry," in which he compares the seventh-century CE Rabbi Joshua b. Perahiah of the rabbinic literature (a legal expert) with the R. Joshua of the magical bowls (a magician) found in Nippur. The latter was, according to Neusner, the view of the common people. See also Berlinerblau, "Popular Religion," for a nuanced analysis of this phenomenon.
112. Dever, "Asherah," 21.
113. Day, "Asherah," 1.483–87.
114. Aḥituv, Eshel, and Meshel, "The Inscriptions," 74.
115. Translations in Aḥituv, Eshel, and Meshel, "The Inscriptions," 87, 95, 98, and 105, respectively.
116. Meshel, "Nature of the Site," 69. There was also a much-publicized drawing of a seated lyre player and two standing figures. Dever (*Ordinary People*, 265; *Did God Have a Wife?*, 164–65) concluded that

northern Israel. The cult stand was constructed in four levels: at the top was a four-footed animal carrying a winged sun. The third level was evidently a doorway to a temple that was empty. This, surmises Dever, represents a male deity who is invisible (Yahweh?). The second level contained two sphinxes (winged lions); the bottom level was made up of two lions with a nude female between them. This female figure, surmises Dever, is undoubtedly Asherah who was known as the "lion lady."[117] If Dever is correct in this interpretation, the point is that once again Asherah seems to be represented along with Yahweh as the goddess of Israel. The common people, therefore, seem to have worshiped Asherah as the consort of Yahweh. Their religion was anything but "orthodox." One should be cautious in extrapolating from two artifacts to conclude that all or most of the common folk were syncretistic in their worship of Yahweh. But it is also striking that these finds, from two different locations (one far to the south and the other in the north), harmonize so well with such a conclusion.

2b. Religion (First-Century CE Asia Minor)

Fast-forward around 800 years to the churches of Galatia in Asia Minor, the recipients of the Apostle Paul's heated letter. Paul wrote to them, "How can you turn back to the weak and poor elementary spirits?" (Gal 4:9). What did he mean by "turn back"? How could these former pagans be turning back? Some 138 Greek inscriptions from Asia Minor, roughly from the same place as the Galatian churches, "both chronologically and geographically,"[118] may offer insights into their ecclesiastical and theological problems. In an essay that seeks to use the inscriptions to clarify the background of the New Testament epistle, Clinton E. Arnold notes a common pattern in the so-called Lydian-Phrygian confessional inscriptions (or, as he prefers, "appeasement" inscriptions):

- Confession of a transgression toward a deity

- Indication of a punishment received (such as blindness, madness, or death of a family member)

the seated figure was a depiction of Asherah. But Beck ("The Drawings," 168, 173), who examined all of the drawings in great detail, does not make that identification.

117. Dever, *Biblical Writers*, 178; Dever, "Asherah"; Dever, *Did God Have a Wife?*, 164–67.
118. See Arnold, "Folk Belief."

- Indication that the anger of the deity has been appeased
- Praise of the deity

These four stages of appeasement are then recorded on a stone *stele*. For example:

> After Diogenes made a vow of his cow to Zeus Peizenos and did not keep it, the god struck the eyes of his daughter Tatiane. But now the god has been propitiated and the stele has been set up.[119]

Arnold argues that the Galatian Christians' preconversion life, living in constant fear of offending a deity due to either cultic or social misdeeds, carried over into their new religious convictions and made it difficult for them to discard cultic obligations. They struggled to understand the grace offered in Paul's religion because it ran counter to everything they had thought up to then. The use of these inscriptions to help the interpreter construct the religious background of the recipients of the Galatian letter is a particularly adept application of literary archaeological remains to the task of biblical interpretation.

3. Economy (First-Century CE Galilee)

"Blessed are you poor, for yours is the Kingdom of God, blessed are you who are hungry . . . but Woe to the rich!" (Luke 6:20, 22, 24). One can get the impression from the New Testament Gospels that Galilee in the first century CE was full of poverty and hunger. But was it? Actually, this topic has sparked a heated debate in recent decades. What is at stake is whether Jesus's ministry was based on socio-economic problems or mostly on religious issues.[120] The two most vocal schools of thought are at the opposite extremes of the issue: One group finds oppressive poverty in first-century CE Galilee; the other group finds a prosperous economy and egalitarian society. Can archaeology help in this discussion? Evidently it cannot help much since both sides look at the same evidence. But here it goes anyway:

What archaeology can show is that there was a rather vigorous manufacture and trade of goods going on in first-century Galilee. This conclusion was first popularized by David Adan-Bayewitz. In a series of publications, he has highlighted the pottery industry of a small vil-

---

119. Translation in Arnold, "Folk Belief," 434.
120. See the survey in Fiensy, *Christian Origins*, 81–97 and Jensen, "Rural Galilee."

lage in the middle of Galilee called Kefar Hananya. Adan-Bayewitz and I. Perlman have established that Kefar Hananya exported its common pottery up to twenty-four kilometers away into Galilee and the Golan. They maintain that 75 percent of the first-century common tablewares excavated at Sepphoris so far (cooking bowls) were made in Kefar Hananya.[121] Further, the survey team of Strange, Groh, and Longstaff established that 15 percent of the storage jars or kraters discovered thus far in Sepphoris originated in the nearby village of Shikhin. The Shikhin storage jars, according to the three archaeologists, account for the majority of pottery of that type in Galilee.[122] The process by which these conclusions were made is called neutron activation analysis. The scientific test allows the excavators to determine the chemical content of the clay used in making the pottery. The clay content of many of the wares found in the villages and cities of Galilee indicates that much of the pottery came from the area of Kefar Hananya and that many of the large jars came from the tiny village of Shikhin (1.5 kilometers from Sepphoris). Adan-Bayewitz concluded, based on his analysis of the pottery distribution:

> [T]he distribution pattern of Kefar Hananya ware does not seem consistent with the picture, common among scholars, of the exploitation in the early Roman period of the Galilean peasant by the urban wealthy.[123]

Thus, Adan-Bayewitz hoped to make socio-economic observations based on his analysis of the pottery. Such a vigorous trade and manufacture meant that the economy of Galilee was humming along and enriching everyone, peasant and elite alike.

Yet, now it appears that the "Kefar Hananya ware" was actually made in many sites in Galilee and not just in that one village center.[124] As a matter of fact, there have now been located six pottery production centers in the Golan from the first century and five in Galilee from the same time period. It appears, as Aviam has pointed out, that those villages where agriculture was challenged due to the terrain, learned to cope economically by initiating industry.[125] These excavations demon-

---

121. See Adan-Bayewitz, *Common Pottery*, 23–41, 216–36; Adan-Bayewitz, "Kefar Hananya"; Adan-Bayewitz and I. Perlman, "Local Trade of Sepphoris."
122. Strange, Groh, and Longstaff, "Excavations at Sepphoris."
123. Adan-Bayewitz, *Common Pottery*, 219.
124. Aviam, "Yodefat," 114; Aviam, "Kefar Hananya Ware."
125. Aviam, "Kefar Hananya Ware," 144. Four of the centers in Galilee listed by Aviam are Kefar Hananya, Shikhin, Karm er-Ras, and Yavor. But now it also appears, by chemical examination of the clays used in the pottery imported to Gadara, that Meiron (in Upper Galilee) was a pottery producer and exporter. See Dazkiewics, Liesen, and Schneider, "Provenance."

strate that there was a vigorous trade of pottery in Galilee in the first century.

There were other industries in Galilee as well. Y. Magen's work on stoneware production has brought to light two quarry workshops in Lower Galilee—one in Bethlehem of Galilee (just southwest of Sepphoris) and the other in Kefar Reina (just east of Sepphoris). These were major producers of stone cups and other vessels. The use of stoneware has been discovered throughout Galilee as well (in twelve villages and cities).[126] In addition, many villages excavated have large installations for olive oil pressing, for wool dyeing, or for cooperages.[127] Industry was thriving in Galilee in the late Second Temple period.

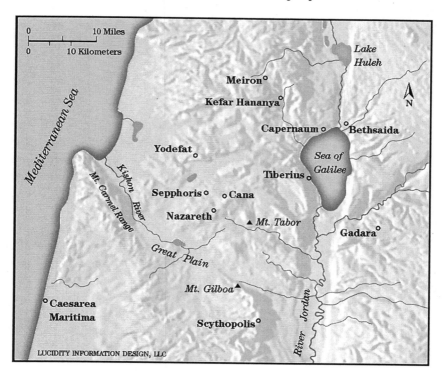

Fig. 2.9 Map of Galilee and the Golan. Used with permission.

---

126. Magen, *Stone Vessel*, 160. The number of villages in which stoneware has been found comes from Magen's 2002 monograph. The count now would be a bit higher as more villages are being excavated.
127. See Fiensy, "Village Life," 194.

So, one cannot doubt that there was a healthy and active trade of goods (pottery, stoneware, olive oil, wool, etc.). But does all the trade indicate a higher standard of living for the average Galilean household? That connection is trickier. We might demonstrate by archaeology that the industry and trade grew the economic pie. But that would not necessarily mean that each household got a larger slice of the pie. That is something archaeology cannot tell us (or has not yet told us). Perhaps prosperity for some also meant poverty for others. As Crossan wisely writes: "What . . . if Antipas's boom *was* Jesus's impoverishment? Ask not for whom the boom booms; it may not boom for thee."[128] In other words (as I would interpret his allusion to John Donne) it is not a simple matter of finding some evidence of increased trade. We need to investigate how such trade affected the average villager. So, here archaeology—so far—cannot settle the issue. Yet it does make a contribution in beginning the conversation.

Conclusion

It is rare that an archaeological find can interpret a single verse or a single text of the Bible. The stones and potsherds do not usually clear up enigmas in the biblical text. The heavens do not open and light does not descend upon a verse of the Bible every time one finds a relic or ruin. Mostly, archaeology provides context or background from which the interpreter can picture the narrative. Indeed, to expect archaeology to be able to interpret individual verses or texts assumes a certain view of scripture: scripture as a collection of propositional statements. Rather, in my view, scripture is more about a story, a metanarrative. Archaeology as context mostly helps us to imagine the story. True, sometimes archaeological remains (or, actually how we interpret the remains) can lead us to disregard part the story as a historical event (as many have done with respect to the exodus). At other times the remains push us to expand the story (as in the cases of the invasions of Shishak and Sennacherib, and the youth of John the Baptist). At times, the remains tell us that the story, as told in scripture, looks historically and culturally plausible. At other times (and mostly I think) the remains just help us get a picture in our minds of "how it was." (What did they eat? Were they ill most of the time? What did they look like? How did they really practice their religion? Were they poor or prosperous?)

128. Crossan, "Relationship," 152.

To imagine the story further, in the next chapters we will join our archaeological data with not only relevant texts but with the discipline of anthropology. First, in chapter 3 we will take a look at how cultural anthropology (mostly ethnographies) can augment the texts and the artifacts. What insights into the ruins and artifacts do we gain by comparing them with contemporary, traditional villages and houses from the Middle East? How can understanding village life in the Iron II period in Israel affect our interpretation of the Hebrew Bible (i.e., help us imagine the story)?

Then, in chapter 4, we enter the discipline of human osteoarchaeology and physical anthropology. We will ask about youth mortality and life expectancy in Israel in the late Second Temple period. These finds will prompt us to think about the social ramifications of high child mortality and short life spans. What would family life be like under those circumstances? How did Israel's average life span compare with those elsewhere in the Greco-Roman world? What might these data mean for our interpretation of the New Testament?

3

All in the Family: House, Family, Village, and Meal in the Iron Age Highlands of Israel

"Yes, wonderful things."[1]

These were the alleged words of Howard Carter in 1922 when he entered King Tutankhamun's tomb in Egypt and was asked if he could see anything. The words summarize what the public has come to expect of archaeology. We want wonderful things and we want them frequently. The "wonderful things" include not only gold from royal tombs (nonexistent in Israel) but monuments from the Israelite period and also "slam dunk" proofs of the historicity of the Bible. This is the common perception of the use of archaeology. These are truly "wonderful things."

But the study of ancient history has taken a few turns in the last decades. No longer is it just about the great politicians and military conquerors. Historians now want to know about the ordinary people. They scan texts now for hints about "everyday life."[2] The same interest

---

1. No Author, "Howard Carter."
2. E.g. Dever, *Ordinary People*; Borowski, *Daily Life*; Hezser, *Oxford Handbook*; King and Stager, *Life in Biblical Israel.*

is also present in Old Testament studies. Old Testament interpreters now ask about the sort of tribal members that would have mustered to fight a battle, the sort of hearers that would have received the Wisdom teachings, the sort of woman written about in Proverbs chapter 31, and the sort of worshipers that would have turned up for ancient Israel's liturgy.[3] In this investigation, archaeology is playing an increasingly significant role.

In the past, interpreters of the Hebrew Bible have been quick to note the convergences of ruins with text. Thus, in the 1981 entry in this series—by the current publisher—Darrell Lance sought to inform the reader of the evidence for the reign of Solomon. He did this by pointing to the similarities in the gates of Gezer, Megiddo, and Hazor and noting that these gates fit stratigraphically with the tenth century BCE. He further suggested evidence in the excavations of Jerusalem for Solomon's reign.[4] This was the emphasis then and is still a very important feature in the archaeological investigation of the Bible. Where these convergences occur between text and ruins, they should be noted (as we did in chapter 2 of this volume). They tell us many things about the nature of the Hebrew Bible.

But increasingly archaeologists and historians want to know more about the ordinary people. Knowing about the monumental ruins of Solomon's reign has its place. But we also now want to know about the ordinary John and Jane Doe (or Yoseph and Rachel) who never visited the royal palace, never conquered foreign foes, and did not leave behind monumental landmarks. How did they live? What was their daily life like? What sort of houses did they inhabit? How did they interact with one another in community? Were they happy?

Some of these questions ("Were they happy?") cannot be answered, at least not by archaeology. One can only guess. But we can make inroads into answering the others. As we noted in chapter 1, we will in this chapter use not just archaeology and the biblical text but cultural anthropology as well. Answering some of these questions may not be as sensational for some readers as were the previous generations' archaeological finds, but the answers get us to the real-life situations for most people of the ancient Israelite world, the world of the Hebrew Bible.

---

3. C. Meyers ("Women's Culture," 427) asks for a bottom-to-top perspective instead of the top-down perspective "that has dominated Syro-Palestinian archaeology."
4. Lance, *Old Testament*, 67–93.

Fig. 3.1 Howard Carter (kneeling), an Egyptian workman, and Arthur Callender at doors of burial shrines in Pharaoh Tutankhamen's tomb. *New York Times* photo archive. Wikimedia Commons.

First, a word about using cultural anthropology for understanding ancient societies (a discipline called ethnoarchaeology). One can certainly abuse or misuse ethnographies of contemporary traditional societies in understanding cultures from three thousand years ago. Naturally, great caution should be the rule. Yet, many archaeologists (mostly those studying the Old Testament; New Testament archaeology has lagged behind in this) now appeal to such studies—ethnographies of premodern[5] Middle Eastern societies—to help reconstruct what was going on in the society that left behind the ruins they have excavated. Lawrence Stager offers the following statement on the use of cultural anthropology:

> At the very least, ethnoarchaeological models, forged from many of the same cultural and ecological constraints operative in the past, provide guidelines within which the archaeologist can reconstruct aspects of everyday life from the patterns of material remains.[6]

In other words, when we view the ruins and scratch our heads wondering how they were used, we might look at traditional societies that have been documented by modern anthropologists/ethnographers for clues. One example, which we will return to below, is the ground floor of the two-story house. It appears that the animals were kept on the first floor of the house based on a few archaeological hints (appearance of mangers and sometimes very low ceilings) and this conclusion is confirmed by appeal to ethnographic studies of the region where keeping animals on the lower floor of the house is common.[7] The ethno-

---

5. See e.g., Dalman, *Haus*, 112–14, 121, 128 who notes the dates of his visits to anthropological informants: between the years 1899 and 1925.
6. Stager, "Archaeology," 18. A common question is, "What does twentieth-century CE rural Iran (e.g.) have to do with Israel in the twelfth through seventh centuries BCE?" There is both a significant time difference and a geographical difference. Even when one cites ethnographic studies of nineteenth- or twentieth-century Palestinian villages, there can be pushed back. Holladay speaks to this issue: "As with other questions involving complex models of operating systems, the best source of insight is the study of similar systems in contemporary societies living at roughly the same stage of development and under most of the same environmental constraints. I.e., we should turn to the sphere of ethnology, particularly that of communities living in similar biospheres, keeping similar domesticates, and following similar subsistence strategies, which in the present case means mixed dry farming employing the simple plow" (Holladay, "House," 312). See also C. Meyers, "Family," 7; C. Meyers, *Rediscovering Eve*, 32–35; Ebeling, *Women's Lives*, 10–12; London, "Ethnoarchaeology"; Labianca, "Everyday Life"; Rosen, "Subsistence Economy," 166, 174, 176; and Hardin, "Understanding Houses," 19–20. Hardin finds "direct ethnographic observations from contemporary settlements located in the same region as the archaeological settlement under investigation" to be very useful but also notes some cautions in the use of cultural anthropology (20).
7. Actually most of the traditional Arab houses had a multi-tiered ground floor with the animals on a lower level and the family on the upper level of the same floor.

graphic studies help the archaeologist decide on the function of the first floor (or ground floor) of the dwelling. It seems most unsanitary and smelly for us westerners to keep your farm animals (sheep, goats, donkeys, oxen, perhaps horses) on the first floor of your house—in other words, for the family to be living on the second floor of an animal barn—and thus obviously (to us) was not done. But the presence of such houses in traditional societies in the Middle East causes us to reconsider. We are better able to take the archaeological evidence for what it seems to be indicating. We will, therefore, cite similar studies below where it seems appropriate to do so.

On the other hand, some knowledge of cultural development over the centuries causes us to know where to disregard the ethnographic data. For example—to stay with the house for a moment—the commonly seen dome-roofed, stone houses in the Middle East and featured in many films on the Bible and in many old photographs and sketches of nineteenth-century Palestine are actually an Islamic innovation introduced in the twelfth century.[8] The Iron Age houses were flat-roofed and mostly constructed of mud bricks.[9] Therefore, whole descriptions of the Palestinian peasants' building of their own stone houses may not be as relevant for Israelite society (though some parts of those descriptions still seem helpful). Thus, one must use caution in applying the ethnographic data. But to ignore it leaves us open to the problem many historians seem to have: ethnocentrism. Without ethnographic informants we tend to interpret the texts and artifacts based on our own experiences and cultural biases.[10]

But our task may require not only the appeal to archaeology, ethnography, and text but to the imagination as well. Being a good historian sometimes forces us to use creative imagination.[11] We need to

---

8. See Fuchs, "Arab House." For other caveats in using ethnographies, see London, "Ethnoarchaeology," 3; Carter, "Ethnoarchaeology."

9. The Arabs still made houses of mud bricks (Canaan called them "clay houses") into the twentieth century, but the majority were made of stone. Canaan's description of these houses is quite relevant to our study. See Canaan, *Arab House*, 54. They also still built houses with flat roofs. See Dalman, *Haus*, 112–17.

10. The following ethnographies were consulted for this chapter: Amiry and Tamari, *Palestinian Village Home*; Canaan, *Arab House*; Dalman, *Haus*; Fuchs, "Arab House"; Fuller, *Buarij*; Hirschfeld, *Palestinian Dwelling*; Kramer, *Village Ethnoarchaeology*; Lutfiyya, *Baytin*; Sweet, *Tell Toqaan*; Tannous, "Arab Village"; and Thompson, *Land*.

11. See Blanton, "Archaeology and the Historical Imagination," who wants to apply the same imagination to the New Testament text: "This brief overview of scholarship is sufficient to indicate that speculation, intuition, and disciplined imagination play at least as large a role in New Testament studies as they do in the interpretation of the artifacts unearthed at any archaeological excavation site." Blanton follows James F. Strange, who calls for the archaeological interpreter to use "disciplined imagination and intuition." See Strange, "Tombs," 400.

feel a bit of empathy for the ancient persons. For example, Peter Oakes has written a work in which he attempts to interpret the New Testament Epistle to the Romans by a look at the architecture of Pompeii, specifically at a block of buildings known as the House of Menander. From the rooms/apartments within the "House of Menander," he constructs a sociological model of craft-workers based on the amount of space each living quarter had. In his model, some workers are comfortable but others live in extremely penurious conditions. In turn he creates four fictional persons who, then, in his imaginative account, read the letter to the Romans from their unique perspective.[12] Thus, the ruins of a "house" or *insula* (block of houses or rooms) helps Oakes to imagine the story of first-century residents of the city of Rome reading Paul's letter. In this way, Oakes wants the ordinary persons of Rome to have a voice. He wants to ask how they might have thought about Paul's great letter to the Romans.

More relevant even than Oakes's work is the monograph of Jennie R. Ebeling. Ebeling constructs a fictional life of a character of her imagination called Orah. She takes Orah from birth to death and explains many things about her life as an adult. Along the way, Ebeling appeals to archaeology, to the biblical text, and to ethnographies to shape an integrated story. She seeks to clarify what life was like for a typical Israelite woman.[13] This is more or less our project in this chapter, though on a more limited basis. We will sketch one day in the life of a fictional couple.

I will, then, attempt to narrate—with commentary—a hypothetical day in the life of a fictional family that lives in a small, rural village in the highlands of Canaan (the Israelite area) in the Iron Age. We will begin with a look at a typical house; outline the basic form of the kinship features of Israelite society; construct an ideal village type based on a composite of several villages from this period; and finally, we will describe the last meal of the day, the large meal where all the family gathered. We may have to use not just archaeology, the biblical text, and ethnographies of similar societies, but also at times our imagination[14] to make the construction.

---

12. Oakes, *Reading Romans*, 96. For a survey of other attempts to interpret the New Testament using architecture and creative imagination, see Blanton, "Archaeology and the Historical Imagination."
13. Ebeling, *Women's Lives*.
14. C. Meyers, "Family," 7: "Material cultural remains are silent resources with respect to human behavior . . . the mute remnants of the past are given voice only through interpretation. Much, if not all, interpretation rests on analogy, often done intuitively."

The House

Our imaginary couple, Yoseph and Rachel (who is both Yoseph's wife and cousin), awaken at dawn in the second floor of their "Four-Room House." They sleep in one of their four second-story rooms.[15] *They have no bed or chair in their room*[16] *but roll out mats*[17] *at night for sleeping. Wealthier houses might have a bed, a table, and a chair in the room (2 Kgs 4:10),*[18] *but these are common rural folk living in a tiny village and they have no luxuries. Yoseph and Rachel roll up their mats, put them in the corner of the room, and awaken their three children sleeping on mats in the same room. There are twelve persons living in their house comprising three generations.*[19] *They have an aging grandfather, the eldest member of the extended family (the grandmother died years ago) who occupies one room, and Yoseph's younger brother, his wife, and their two children who occupy a room together.*[20] *They also have living in their house Yoseph's fifteen-year-old concubine and their new baby.*[21]

15. Dever, *Ordinary People*, 131 observes that these houses had on the second story from four to eight rooms.
16. Wright, "Israelite Daily Life," 61; Dever, *Ordinary People*, 169. For the ordinary houses nothing remains of furniture or for that matter of eating utensils. People, as Dever concludes, evidently ate sitting on the floor and with their hands. This conclusion is confirmed by the ethnographic data. See Canaan, *Arab House*, 48; Hirschfeld, *Palestinian Dwelling*, 120–34; Amiry and Tamari, *Palestinian Village*, 25–29; Sweet, *Tell Toqaan*, 131. These works observe that the Palestinian "peasants" or poor farmers had no furniture in their houses. Dalman (*Haus*, 114) wrote of one house he visited: "Everything was done squatting, sitting, or lying on the bare floor." These people, wrote Dalman, were accustomed to the hard floors (176).
17. Dalman, *Haus*, 176 observed mats in his day (from the late nineteenth through the early twentieth centuries) in Palestine and Syria made from papyrus, reed, rushes, and hemp. To have a rug, wrote Dalman, was a step up.
18. See Ps 63:7 [Eng. 6], 132:3; and Job 17:13 for couches יצוע and 1 Sam 19:13, 15–16; 2 Sam 4:7; 1 Kgs 17:19 for beds מטה.
19. Faust and Bunimovitz, "Four Room House," 26; *pace* Stager, "Archaeology," 18 who thought only four to five persons on average lived in these houses. Dever, *Ordinary People*, 131, 132, 151, 154, 157, and 201 seems to agree with the larger family size although in places Dever seems back and forth on the number of individuals in a family inhabiting a typical, rural-village, four-room house. See also Shiloh, "Population," 29 who offers an average of eight members per household; and Schloen, *House*, 136 (followed by Adams, *Social and Economic Life*, 15) who believes that the average household contained ten members. C. Meyers (*Rediscovering Eve*, 111) suggests as many as fifteen persons living in a rural village house and notes ethnographic data from Palestine/Israel indicating that as many as sixteen lived in Arab houses.
20. Faust and Bunimovitz, "Four Room House," 26.
21. For the concubine idea, see Ebeling, *Women's Lives*, 27. C. Meyers (*Rediscovering Eve*, 109) believes only the elite had more than one wife. It is true that most of the time (except for Samuel's father, 1 Sam 1:2), polygyny is narrated with reference to elite families. But not much in general is said about common rural folk (see Hamilton, "Marriage," 565). The fact that Deuteronomy must later regulate having two wives in one nuclear family (Deut 21:15–17) argues that this social situation existed long before the law. One could imagine here that the concubine was an אמה, a "maidservant" or "concubine" (see Holladay, *Lexicon*, 19). She might have been like the אמה of Exod 21:7–11 who was sold to a family as a girl with the understanding that she would be married to one of the sons when she reached adulthood (Garroway, *Children*, 130–34).

Fig. 3.2 Women sitting Arab house at turn of last century. Used by permission of Georg Olms Verlag. In Dalman, *Haus*, photo 35. The house was in the village of *Balat* in north Palestine and he visited it in 1900. The women sit on the floor preparing vegetables. One can see one of the pillars of the house on the right and on the far right the bedding folded up. Notice the presence of what was often lacking in these houses, according to Dalman: a window.

Yoseph and Rachel have three children[22] and she is now pregnant again for the seventh time. In the fourteen years of their marriage, Rachel has suffered one miscarriage and given birth to five children, of which two have died.[23] Two of

22. Demographic studies of nuclear families (husband, wife, and their children) have indicated that there is an average of around five persons per family. See Laslett, "Mean Household"; and Hayami and Uchida, "Size of Household." I am assuming a nuclear family for Yoseph and Rachel of five persons and a total extended family size in the house of twelve. But, of course, family size was dynamic: There were births, deaths, and marriages of female children that added and subtracted from the number.

23. C. Meyers, "Family," 28; ibid., *Rediscovering Eve*, 98–99, 109–10; and see chapter 4 of this volume. C. Meyers, (*Rediscovering Eve*, 99, 110) estimates that each woman on average had eight pregnancies in her lifetime, giving birth to six children of which 50 percent survived. Dever, *Ordinary People*, 201, suggests that the typical woman would give birth to "a dozen" children plus suffering numerous miscarriages and that only three or four of these twelve live births would survive childhood. These figures are drastically different from those I will present in chapter 4. He does not state on what basis he makes these suggestions. Stager ("Archaeology," 18) on the other hand, states that each family produced six children of which only two survived. Again, he does not indicate the evidence for his figures. Angel, "Ecology," 95, found in his data (based on only seven individuals) that the average births per female in the Iron Age Eastern Mediterranean world was 4.1 and the average survival of those live births was 1.9. One hesitates in this case to give Angel's otherwise

the surviving children are girls (ages thirteen and three) and her son is nine years old. Her elder daughter will soon be given to some young man in the village for a wife.[24]

Yoseph and Rachel use one of the second-story rooms (the largest one) as their sleeping/living/dining room; the grandfather uses a second, small room; his brother and family use the third room; the concubine and her new baby use the fourth (very small) room; and the rest of the second floor is for storage.

It seems improbable to westerners that the couple would sleep in the same room as the children, but ethnographic studies from the Middle East show us that this is what traditional folk prefer.[25] The nuclear family (parents and children) share one room within the larger house of a perhaps multigenerational extended family (I am supposing three generations in our hypothetical house).

Rachel does not feel well most days. Not only is she almost perpetually either pregnant or nursing a child, but unknown to her, she has contracted intestinal parasites.[26] *Her intestines are full of whipworms contracted from handling animal fecal remains. These parasites compete with her own system for the nourishment she takes into her body and make her feel exhausted.*[27] *Most days she is tired not only from her pregnancy or her breastfeeding of a baby, and from her medical condition (the intestinal parasites), but also from her endless toil from dawn to dark. She is now twenty-eight years old and will live only four or five more years.*[28]

---

valuable pioneering work too much credulity in light of such small sample sizes. Kramer, *Village Ethnoarchaeology*, 24, reported that the average female in her studied village gave birth to 4.9 children. C. Meyers ("Archaeology," 77) surmises that "if not infertile, women were pregnant or nursing for much of their adult life."

24. See Huebner, "Mediterranean Family," 13, who notes that throughout the Mediterranean world in antiquity (she lists specifically Rome, Athens, and Egypt) girls married in their mid-teens. The rabbinic texts indicate the same for the Jewish girls of Palestine. See Strack and Billerbeck, *Kommentar*, 2.373–75. Gallant, *Risk*, 18–19, agrees that girls married in their mid-teens in ancient Greece but perhaps late teens in the first two centuries of the Roman imperial world.

25. See Holladay, "House," 314, who cites ethnographic studies from western Iran: "Each nuclear family had its own living room. There the family ate, slept, did indoor work, and entertained." Other ethnographers who refer to this practice are: Dalman, *Haus*, 77; Canaan, *Arab House*, 59; Hirschfeld, *Palestinian Dwelling*, 120–34; and Fuchs, "Arab House," 160. Dever, *Ordinary People*, 156–57, assumes that the married couples had a room on the upper floor separate from the children and that the extended family shared a large common room for dining and entertaining. His suggestions seem ethnographically uninformed. Hirschfeld reports the response of one *mukhtar* to the question: How could the husband and wife have sex with everyone in the same room? The *mukhtar* answered, "It was done by stealth" (*Palestinian Dwelling*, 134).

26. Harter, Mumcuoglu, and Zias, "Toilet Practices"; Mitchell and Tepper, "Intestinal Parasitic Worm Eggs"; Edward Neufeld, "Hygiene Conditions"; Zias, "Death and Disease"; Cahill, et al., "It Had to Happen." See chapter 2 of this volume.

27. For the nutritional needs of pregnant women, see C. Meyers, *Rediscovering Eve*, 53–54.

28. See Dever, *Ordinary People*, 201, who gives the average life span of a female as thirty years and of a male as forty years. C. Meyers, *Rediscovering Eve*, 99, suggests between thirty and forty for men and between twenty and thirty for women. Angel, "Ecology," 94, gives an average life span for the Iron Age Eastern Mediterranean region as 38.8 for males and 30.4 for females. I assume rela-

But there is no time to rest today. She must be up and laboring. The bread-making alone (grinding, kneading dough, heating the oven, and baking) will consume two to three hours of her time.[29] Then she must attend to the spinning, to the weaving, perhaps to pottery making, to cooking the supper, and to the three-year-old toddler (though her elder daughter will also help in that). She may also have to care for an aging family member. She will tend to the garden and milk[30] the sheep and goats (who await her downstairs on the ground floor).[31] During harvest she and the children also work in the fields.[32] She averages working ten hours per day.[33]

Rachel's husband, Yoseph, labors intensively as well but with less drain on his energy in the winter months. There is always work to do in plowing, planting, weeding, and harvesting (including mowing, threshing, and winnowing). He may have to clear new fields of stones and trees. He might have to hew out new cisterns or help someone in the village build his house. He will probably have to construct terraces or keep them in repair. He will also tend to olive and other fruit orchards. In addition, he must keep the house repaired and his tools repaired. His life span will probably be a bit longer than his wife's (by four or five years) but he is also four years older than she.[34]

The children have also started working (they started at age five[35]). The younger children water animals, glean in the fields, run errands for their mother, help care for elderly family members, and gather firewood (Jer 7:18).[36] The older children work alongside adults, the girls making bread and watching

---

tively similar mortality rates in the Iron Age as in the Late Hellenistic-Early Roman periods and thus would attribute an average life span for females as thirty-three years and for males as thirty-seven years. See chapter 4 of this volume. Cf. MacDonald, *Israelites Eat?*, 86 who suggests an average life expectancy for both sexes as 36.9 years.

29. C. Meyers, "Family," 25 suggests breadmaking took two hours a day (which she clarifies in *Rediscovering Eve*, 130, as just the grinding time). MacDonald, *Israelites Eat?*, 21 thinks it took three hours a day on average. Ebeling, *Women's Lives*, 48 offers that, based on her reading of ethnographies, breadmaking took up to five hours each day.

30. According to Borowski, *Every Living Thing*, 46, the milking season in Israel is from December/January to June/August.

31. C. Meyers, "Family," 25. See Prov 31:10–24. See also C. Meyers, "Women's Culture," 431, and Ebeling, *Women's Lives*, 46, who note that these work obligations for women are common in 185 societies examined around the world.

32. See C. Meyers, *Rediscovering Eve*, 51, and Ebeling, "Engendering," for some ethnographic and literary examples of women sharing the agricultural duties with men.

33. Carol Meyers's estimate ("Family," 25).

34. C. Meyers, "Family," 24. See also chapter 4 of this volume.

35. C. Meyers, "Family," 27. But see *Rediscovering Eve*, 137 where she suggests age six as the start of work for children. Garroway, *Children*, 143, notes that some Ancient Near Eastern legal texts refer to age five as the start of work for children (who have been sold as slaves) but opines that it really depended on the individual child. She suggests that somewhere between the ages of four and six a child was considered able to work. Naomi Steinberg (*World of the Child*, 78–80) found that age four to five was a transition in the Israelite life cycle. Lev 27:5–6 seems to make age five a turning point in childhood.

36. King and Stager, *Life in Biblical Israel*, 65; Garroway, *Children*, 45; C. Meyers, *Rediscovering Eve*, 52.

the babies of the family; the boys out in the fields carrying rocks, plowing, planting, harvesting, and taking care of the sheep and goats.[37]

By age thirteen (or adulthood), children are doing a full day's work like an adult.[38] There was no childhood as we know it. For most children, as a matter of fact, until modern times, their "childhood" was one of work, either on a farm or in a factory. Did they play games as children do now? One would think that they must have but they also worked as much as they were physically capable in a day.[39] Most adult men, if given the choice, will not tend to the sheep and goats in the Middle East, as it is viewed as beneath them. Either boys are given that task or men of low class.[40]

Rachel and Yoseph descend from their second-floor room by way of the external stone stairs.[41] *There they are greeted (in the winter) by the bleating of the sheep and goats and the braying of the ox and perhaps the donkey. The female sheep and goats need to be milked and all of the animals need to be fed by placing hay or straw in their mangers. The side rooms of the ground floor of their "Four Room House" are for animals. The larger central room is where many of the labor activities take place (grinding flour, kneading dough, baking in ovens in the winter—in hot summer months they use the ovens outside in the courtyard—and other activities).*

The designation "Four Room House" has been the description of these houses since the seminal publication of Yigal Shiloh,[42] but now scholars prefer to call them the "pillared house" since some of them—especially those in the cities—had less than four rooms (usually three).[43] The more than 150 of these houses from this time period excavated indicate that this house style persisted as the predominant floor

---

37. Ebeling, *Women's Lives*, 46.
38. C. Meyers, "Family," 27. But C. Meyers (*Rediscovering Eve*, 137) later opines that they begin at age ten to work as an adult. Cf. Scheidel, "Real Wages"; and Garroway, *Children*, 155–58, for hiring out children in Roman Egypt and in the Ancient Near East respectively.
39. Children growing up in Mesopotamia had toys. See Garroway, *Children*, 46.
40. Fuller, *Buarij*, 45; Lutfiyya, *Baytin*, 28, 30. When grown men are forced by economic necessity to tend sheep and goats, they are often made fun of. The author has observed that in Jordan today, the herders of sheep and goats in a village may often be Iraqi refugees. They are considered the lowest class. Even the boys do not like doing it evidently. Fuller (45) observed that the job was often given to a wayward son, to a dullard, or to an orphan. On the other hand, Borowski (*Every Living Thing*, 48) points out that the Bedouin (i.e., those not tied to a village) use young girls for tending the sheep and goats. The girls continue in this task until marriage. In the Hebrew Bible, one can find references both to unmarried girls tending goats (Rebecca, Rachel, and Leah) and to boys (David).
41. Wright, "Israelite Daily Life," 60. Wright opines that some houses used wooden stairs but nothing of them has remained. See also Holladay, "House," 309. The stone stairs have survived in many of the Iron Age houses.
42. Shiloh, "Four Room House."
43. Stager, "Archaeology"; Faust, "Rural Community"; Dever, *Ordinary People*, 128; C. Meyers, "Family," 14. See the numerous house plans listed in Braemer, *L'Architecture*, 39–101 with comments. He

plan throughout the Iron I and Iron II periods (1200–586 BCE).[44] Thus the house plan is very well known. The floor plan, for most of the small, rural, village houses, consisted of three long rooms divided by two rows of pillars and a broad room in the back of the house. Below is a composite of the standard plan of a first floor of a pillared Iron Age house in Israel:[45]

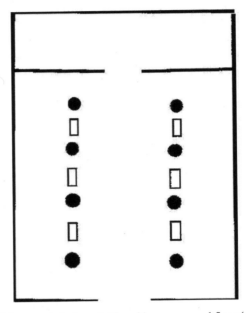

Fig. 3.3 Theoretical (composite) plan of pillared house, ground floor (Iron Age). Illustration by author. This basic plan was capable of several variations as Braemer, *L'Architecture*, 43 illustrates. The theoretical plan given here is taken from Braemer's Type III category (the four-room houses) with the addition of the mangers.

The reader will note on the first floor of the house the presence of mangers.[46] Most archaeologists now think that the first floor was used for stalling animals at night (only in winter?) and for storage.[47] The side

organizes them into four types (two rooms to five rooms). Netzer, "Domestic Architecture," 197, prefers to call these "long-spaced houses."

44. Holladay, "House," 308; Bunimovitz and Faust, "Ideology in Stone," 34. Actually this is an old figure (the number excavated by the year 1987).

45. For several floor plans of Iron Age pillared houses, see Stager, "Archaeology," 15; Faust and Bunimovitz, "Four Room House," 23; Holladay, "House," 311; Dever, *Ordinary People*, 130; and Braemer, *L'Architecture*, 43.

46. See Stager, "Archaeology," 13–14.

47. Dever, *Ordinary People*, 129; Stager, "Archaeology," 14; C. Meyers, "Family," 15; Netzer, "Domestic Architecture," 198 and n. 17.

rooms would have been for the animals and the center room for daily activities. In the center rooms have been found ovens, mortars and pestles, large storage jars, grinding stones, cisterns, jugs, cooking pots, dishes, bins, and probably grain pits.[48] The center rooms usually have floors of packed earth while the side rooms might be paved with flagstones.[49] Further, some of the ceiling heights of the first floor of these houses—when they can be determined from adequate remains—seem uncomfortably small, even in light of the smaller stature of persons in the Iron Age (see chapter 4). One house had a ceiling of only 3'7", far too short for people even then but adequate for animals. Most of the ceilings of the first floor ranged from 5'3" to 6'6".[50] These ceiling heights indicate something of the stature of these people but also that there is no waste of building materials. They built the walls only as high as absolutely necessary. Lower walls also make the second story more stable. The walls of these houses were usually constructed from a bottom course or two of stones followed by rows of sun-dried mud bricks.[51] The bricks were constructed by mixing mud with straw and sand and then placing them in rectangular molds to dry. The walls were then plastered, inside and outside, with mud-chaff plaster to seal out the wind and perhaps (?) insects.[52]

Noting that the animals spent nights in the family's house, King and Stager surmise that this practice explains the idea of the "fatted calf." The fatted calf is actually the stall-fed calf, the calf that is not allowed out of doors but only fed in the house.[53]

That the animals spent the night on the first floor of the house stalled in the side rooms is also attested in ethnographic studies. Both anthropologists and travelers report that many traditional Arab houses brought the animals into the house at night, especially in the winter.[54]

48. Wright, "Israelite Daily Life," 60; C. Meyers, "Field Crops to Food," 71; Stager, "Archaeology," 11–13. Most of Stager's data seem to come from three excavations: 'Ai, Raddana, and Giloh (11). For grain storage pits, see Currid and Navon, "Iron Age Pits."

49. Stager, "Archaeology," 12; Holladay, "House," 309; Netzer, "Domestic Architecture," 198; Braemer, L'Architecture, 138. Braemer points out that rarely other flooring materials have been discovered through excavation: bricks, pebbles, and plaster.

50. Stager, "Archaeology," 11. See also Wright, "Israelite Daily Life," 60; Holladay, "House," 309. Netzer, "Domestic Architecture," 198 observes that the combined height of both stories was usually between 4 and 5m (13 to 16 feet).

51. Dalman, Haus, 10, suggested that stone houses were for the wealthy. See Isa 9:9 [Eng 9:10]; Amos 5:11.

52. Holladay, "House," 309; Dever, Ordinary People, 131; Borowski, Daily Life, 20; King and Stager, Life, 28.

53. Stager, "Archaeology," 15; King and Stager, Life, 34. See also 1 Sam 28:24, Amos 6:4, Ps 50:9, Jer 46:21, Mal 3:20 (Eng 4:2), and Luke 15:23–27.

54. See Dever, Ordinary People, 131; Stager, "Archaeology," 14; Borowski, Every Living Thing, 45; Borowski, Daily Life, 19 and 130, note 29: "We could have slept in the largest of the houses, but

The heat from the larger animals would elevate the temperatures for the rooms on the second floor and it would offer some protection against having one's animals stolen. Evidently, the animal odors would have been a matter of indifference to the human residents.[55]

Compare our hypothetical pillared house with the floor plan of one below excavated at 'Izbet Ṣarṭah, about fifteen kilometers (nine miles) east of Tel Aviv. This house from the Iron I period and comprising part of a one-hundred-member village, is about the size of our hypothetical house.

The floor space of the ground floor averaged around 1200 square feet. I arrive at this average size based both on the general statements of archaeologists[56] and on specific data presented in the literature. Avraham Faust, for example, gives the dimensions of twenty Iron Age houses from three villages in northern Israel (Samaria). The average size of the twenty houses was 1165 square feet with the smallest house being 861 square feet and the largest 1442 square feet. He also notes that in the villages there is usually very little difference in the size of the houses (though village houses tended to be larger than city houses). There seems to have been a standard size that everyone followed in each village.[57]

We will suggest that our hypothetical floor plan above has the dimensions 42 ft. × 29 ft. (1218 square feet) with a ceiling height of 5'10" (see above). Even allowing that the family lived and slept only on the upper story (assuming that the second story kept the same dimensions as the ground floor), this size fits the usual conclusion about how many square feet per person the ancients required: 100 square feet per

---

there were some little drawbacks; it was populous with vermin, it had a dirt floor, it was in no respect cleanly, and there was a family of goats in the only bedroom, and two donkeys in the parlor" (quoting Mark Twain who traveled to Palestine in the nineteenth century). Other ethnographic reports of the first floor of the house (or in many Arab houses, the lower level of the same room) being reserved for the livestock can be found in: Dalman, *Haus*, 121, 123, 129; Hirschfeld, *Palestinian Dwelling*, 120–34; Canaan, *Arab House*, 45; Fuchs, "Arab House," 158 (who calls the lower floor the "soiled area"); Kramer, *Village Ethnoarchaeology*, 106; Lutfiyya, *Baytin*, 20; Fuller, *Buarij*, 8; Tannous, "Arab Village Community," 529. Tannous writes: "It seems that the idea of a separate barn has never taken root in that part of the world" (529).

55. Note the nineteenth-century report of Thompson, *Land*, 2.544: "The houses are not fit to put pigs in, and every door-yard is full of mire and filth."

56. Faust, "Rural Community," 19; Faust and Bunimovitz, "Four Room House," 26; Dever, *Ordinary People*, 132. Schloen, *House*, suggests 1076 square feet as standard. Clark, "Bricks," 36 suggests 1000 to 1300 square feet as typical. Hardin (*Lahav II*, 196) makes the average house size between 860 and 1722 square feet. C. Meyers, *Rediscovering Eve*, 106, offers 1050 to 1400 square feet as typical.

57. Faust, *Archaeology*, 130–40. See also Dever's two detailed presentations of houses from Tell Halif and Kh. Er-Ras (*Ordinary People*, 149–60), which had around 975 and 1300 square feet on the ground floor respectively. See also the plan of the house from 'Izbet Ṣarṭah above (with 1316 square feet).

person of living space.[58] I assume that the second story had the same square footage as the ground floor.

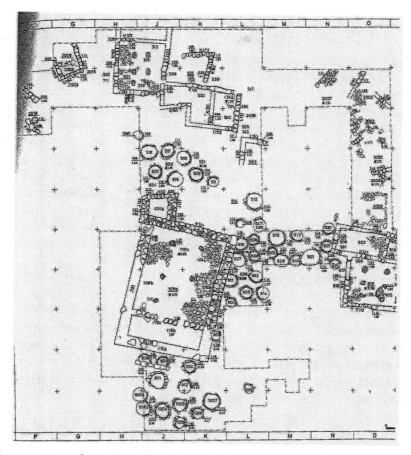

Fig. 3.4 House 109 from 'Izbet Ṣarṭah. The inside dimensions of the house provided 1316 square feet. Notice the two rows of three columns each, which divide the side rooms from the central room. This house had an extra small room attached on the north side. The door is in the northwest corner. Finkelstein, 'Izbet Ṣarṭah, 14–15. A structure with two rows of three pillars each was also common in premodern Arab houses. See Dalman, Haus, 122, 128. Reproduced with permission of BAR publishing.

58. See Stager, "Archaeology," 18; Dever, Ordinary People, 132; and Faust and Bunimovitz, "Four Room House," 30. This ratio of living space to persons is confirmed ethnographically by studies from western Iran. Holladay notes that these studies show that the families average $21m^2$ per person (226 square feet) of total space, including stables for animals and storage rooms. Thus, the living and animal stabling space together are twice the figure customarily used for only the living space of ancient houses. This ethnographic evidence, then, confirms the standard figure used by most archaeologists. See Holladay, "House," 312.

The ground floor is divided into three areas by the two rows of pillars (with interspersing mangers). These pillars can be either monoliths or made up of blocks or drums of stone[59] (perhaps occasionally wooden). Holladay notes that the load-bearing capacity of these pillars is usually more than one would need just for a roof.[60] Thus, I presume, they testify to a second story.[61] The survival of stone stairs in some excavated houses also attests to a second story. Placed usually between the pillars (sometimes on "stub walls" or platforms[62]) were shallow troughs, evidently mangers. These are similar to installations attested as mangers in stables at Beersheba and Hazor.[63]

The central area (room) would have been the largest room with the side rooms (i.e., the animal stalls) the narrowest. The central room was the site of the daily indoor labor, especially in winter. In times past, archaeologists thought this room was left unroofed, forming a sort of open courtyard.[64] But most today believe it was also roofed.[65] Here would be the oven and hearth for cooking in the winter. In the hot summer months, the cooking would have been done in the outside courtyard.[66]

The entry into the ground floor of the house, usually into the central room or area, was through a wooden door set into sockets that were carved both into the lintel and the threshold. The threshold was usually one block of stone. On the lintel and the doorposts of the Israelite houses in Egypt, the Israelites were said (Exod 12:7) to have smeared the blood of the Passover lamb to ward off the death angel. Sometimes the doors would be fitted with a kind of primitive lock and unbolted with a large wooden key (see Song of Sol 5:4–6; Judg 3:24–25).[67]

The windows, according to King and Stager, were little more than slits in the wall. They had no glass in them but were useful for letting in a bit of light and air. Most importantly, the windows served as exhaust vents for the fires in the hearths and ovens built in the central room of the ground floor. There were no chimneys evidently (none have been

59. See the illustrations in Braemer, L'Architecture, 125, 127.
60. Holladay, "House," 309.
61. So Netzer, "Domestic Architecture," 198.
62. Also called stylobates.
63. Holladay, "House," 309.
64. See, e.g., Wright, "Daily Life," 60.
65. See Stager, "Archaeology," 15; and Faust and Bunimovitz, "Four Room House," 23.
66. See C. Meyers, "Field Crops," 71, who also notes that baking bread can be done on a ceramic or iron griddle placed over an open fire (the hearth; Lev 2:5, 7; 7:9). She also observes that some ovens, larger than needed for a single family, may have been used communally by the village. Such a practice accords with ethnographic studies as well. See Tannous, "Arab Village Community," 534.
67. King and Stager, Life, 30–32. See an artist's sketch of the lock on p. 33.

found in the ruins) and thus the smoke from these fires had to find its way out through the small windows.[68] Not only would the smoke irritate the eyes and mucous membranes, but it would eventually soot up the interior of the lower level of the house and make for a very dark environment.[69]

The broad room or backroom was in the past assumed to be the living/sleeping/dining room for the family. Today it is usually thought of as a storage room.[70] A broad room excavated at Shechem contained a stone-lined pit at one end of the room as well as a grain silo. King and Stager conclude that this room was a "pantry."[71] It appears that the broad room was often used for storage.

The second story was used for living space. Each nuclear family, as we stated above, would have had its own room used for everything that we now use our entire houses for in the western world: as a dining room, a living room, and a bedroom. There are numerous references to these second stories called עליה (ʿaliyyah) in the Hebrew Bible: Eglon sat in his ʿaliyyah when Ehud assassinated him (Judg 3:20). Elijah brought the dead boy to the ʿaliyyah (1 Kgs 17:19). Ahaziah fell through the lattice in his ʿaliyyah (2 Kgs 1:2). A woman of means made a room in the ʿaliyyah for Elisha (2 Kgs 4:10).[72] The upper story was cooler in summer and perhaps in the winter helped the residents escape some of the barn odors emanating from below when the livestock were stalled there.[73]

The roof on the second story was made of branches with thatch and mud plaster. The roof required continual maintenance, especially during and just after the rainy season to keep the mud smoothed down. Archaeologists have found stone roof rollers in some houses indicating the ancient method of maintaining their roofs. There is also ethnographic evidence that roof rollers were used in traditional villages in the recent past.[74]

---

68. King and Stager, *Life*, 30.
69. Canaan, *Arab House*, 62, reported this typical feature in Arab houses but wrote that some would leave a small hole in the roof of the house to vent the smoke. See also Dalman, *Haus*, 55–56, who observed the same result in the Arab houses he visited. Dalman wrote that in many of the village houses, there were no windows at all (112–13), evidently to prevent robbery. But some of them had small round windows (he calls them "hatches") higher up on the wall and others had holes in the roof/ceiling for smoke exhalation (74, 128).
70. Holladay, "House," 310; C. Meyers, *Rediscovering Eve*, 107.
71. King and Stager, *Life*, 35.
72. See Stager, "Archaeology," 16. The Greek equivalent was apparently υπερωον. See Acts 9:37.
73. Arabs in premodern times used the roofs of their one-story houses for summer sleeping. Often, according to Dalman (*Haus*, 58–59) they built a small hut for summer and for hosting guests.
74. Dever, *Ordinary People*, 131; Borowski, *Daily Life*, 20; Wright, "Israelite Daily Life," 60. Ethnographically, see Canaan, *Arab House*, 48, 54–55; Hirschfeld, *Palestinian Dwelling*, 120–34; Sweet, *Tell Toqaan*, 114–15; and Thompson, *Land*, 1.132, 386; 2.434.

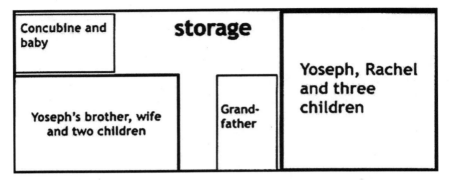

Fig. 3.5 Suggested living/sleeping/eating space on the second floor of our hypothetical Israelite house. Illustration by author.

Yoseph and his brother built the house themselves with a little help now and then from their more distant relatives and neighbors in the village. They learned how to build houses from their parents and other family members. They first gathered the materials: stones for the foundations, lime for plaster (burning limestone produces lime); dirt piles for making mud plasters, wooden beams and smaller branches for the ceiling and roof. They used the counsel of an experienced builder in the beginning of the process, someone in their village, but the labor was done by them and by the women and children. The women and children gathered stones to burn for lime and smaller sticks for the roof.[75] They then set the stones in a trench for a foundation and began making bricks (mud mixed with chopped straw and set in molds to dry in the sun).[76]

Ethnographers report that in contemporary Middle Eastern cultures, each household builds its own house but that distant relatives and neighbors pitch in and help. This is especially true if someone has a special expertise or skill to contribute. In one village, it is the custom for everyone to assist the household and to finish the house building in only a few days.[77] One can easily imagine a similar custom in Iron Age Israel with all the cousins contributing labor and expertise.

The artist's reconstruction below offers an accurate depiction of the pillared house:

75. Cf. the ethnographic evidence of Canaan, *Arab House*, 12–25, 54–55; Hirschfeld, *Palestinian Dwelling*, 113, 115, 118, 120, 217–19, 222; Amiry and Tamari, *Palestinian Village*, 20 for women and children helping in constructing a dwelling.
76. See Canaan, *Arab House*, 54; Clark, "Bricks," 41; and Homsher, "Mud Bricks."
77. See Kramer, *Village Ethnoarchaeology*, 94, and Sweet, *Tell Toqaan*, 117. Clark, "Bricks," 38, maintains that it would take four men and a donkey around one month to construct a stone foundation story for a brick house.

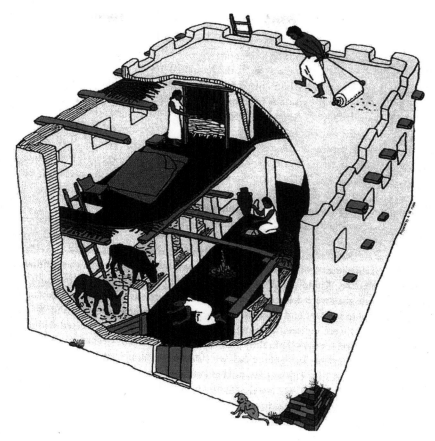

Fig. 3.6 Reconstruction of pillared Iron Age house. © Lawrence E. Stager. Used with permission. King and Stager, *Life in Biblical Israel*, 29. This reconstruction is very frequently reproduced.

T. Canaan wrote that a new house in traditional Palestinian culture was considered unhealthy for the first year since it remained damp (because the walls were so thick). There was a saying among the peasants: "The first year [give your house] to your enemy, the second to your neighbor and the third [keep it] for yourself."[78] One can believe that the ancient houses were equally damp and unhealthy for the first year or so.

The smaller children are put to work bringing in hay for the animals and collecting sticks and animal manure to burn in the oven. Later in the day they

78. Canaan, *Arab House*, 49.

run errands for their mother. The women and older children begin milking the sheep and goats and then they open the front door to let the animals outside for the day.[79] There is no breakfast as such. They are given a morsel of bread left over from the night before. The children consume some of the milk immediately after it is produced from the sheep and goats.[80] Workers wandering out into the fields take snacks with them for later (parched wheat or barley and some fruit). The main meal will be at the end of the day.[81]

The Family

The brothers and the grandfather work together on their farm. Together they keep the house repaired and waterproofed, they plow and plant the fields, and they tend to the livestock. The two sons, one of Yoseph who is nine and one of Yoseph's younger brother who is six, help herd the sheep and goats each day. This is the "house(hold) of the father" of the Hebrew Bible. The "father"[82] (our widowed grandfather) is the oldest male member of the household. Upon his death, the two nuclear families will break up, with the younger son building his own house.

If the inhabitants of this house are as most exegetes and archaeologists now think, they formed the biblical בית אב (bēt 'av) "house(hold) of the father" or extended family.[83] Avraham Faust and Shlomo Bunimovitz believe that extended families ("houses or households of the father") tended in the Iron Age to live together in the same "pillared house."[84] The house sizes fit with this hypothesis and as they point out,

---

79. See King and Stager, *Life in Biblical Israel*, 46; and Garroway, *Children*, 45, for typical children's duties.
80. King and Stager (*Life in Biblical Israel*, 67) suggest that the Israelites ate three meals a day but that the first meal was very meager (bread and fruit) and that the second meal was perhaps bread, olives, and figs. The main meal was in the evening. In spite of MacDonald's assertion that people did not drink fresh milk, common sense would seem to dictate otherwise. See *Israelites Eat?* 35. MacDonald does have some ethnographic support for his conclusion. See Luftiyya, *Baytin*, 114; and Judges 4:19.
81. Borowski, *Daily Life*, 74.
82. Here because of the debate over the role of the oldest male of the *bet 'av*. King and Stager, *Life in Biblical Israel*, 38, affirm that Israelite families were patriarchal and maintain that the oldest male was the *pater familias* like that of the Roman culture who had power over the entire family, the wife, the children, and the slaves. (But King and Stager assert that the power of the Israelite father was not absolute since, for example, children were protected: Deut 21:18–21). C. Meyers, "Patriarchal," maintains that although Israelite families were patrilineal and patrilocal, they were not patriarchal. She further wants to regard him as the "senior male" and to conclude that he shared authority with the senior female of the extended family (private correspondence). Christine Garroway, on the other hand, follows the view of King and Stager and believes that Israelite families were patriarchal, referring to the head of the *bet 'av* as the *pater familias* (*Children*, 134, 172, 174). I will keep the neutral term "grandfather" and not attempt in this short chapter to decide the question.
83. There are also four references to a *bet 'em* or "house of the mother" in the Hebrew Bible. See C. Meyers, "Family," 34; and Ebeling, *Women's Lives*, 28.

most of the rural, village houses were about the same size (1200 square feet on each floor).[85] A nuclear family of five persons does not need so large a house. Thus, the house size is consistent with a presumption that most Israelites lived in an extended, multigenerational family (called ubiquitously in the Hebrew Bible bēt 'av[86]). The "father" of the house was the grandfather of the family. After his death, presumably the oldest son became the new "father" of the house and the other sons moved out.

According to Sabine Huebner, three factors have historically inclined Mediterranean families to live together in multigenerational arrangements: first, where the population density is great and land is scarce; second, where the family engages in farming for subsistence; and third, where the society determines that all male heirs must inherit at least a part of the estate.[87] Living together as an extended family—and thus keeping the estate in one piece—in these situations makes good economic sense and helps guarantee survival (subsistence). At least two of these conditions prevailed in Israel in the Iron I and II ages and further support the premise of extended families being the norm for ancient Israel.

As the family leaves their house, they walk out into the courtyard. It is not their courtyard exclusively but they share it with their somewhat more distant relatives, the family of their grandfather's brother. As a matter of fact, they share not only the courtyard but they share also one of their walls with the brother's family. They greet their second and third cousins (one of whom is married to their sister) and walk off together into their fields to work.

Some archaeologists have noted that in a few spots in the villages, houses share a wall with each other and evidently they shared a common outer courtyard. These "compounds" were, surmise the archaeologists, family units. Stager[88] and Brody[89] have collected some examples of compounds and sought to infer family relationships from them. They look something like the following:

---

84. Faust, "Rural Community," 20–21; Faust and Bunimovitz, "Four Room House," 26. Hardin, *Lahav*, 196, and Schloen, *House*, 150, agree.
85. Faust and Bunimovitz, "Four Room House," 30n5.
86. See e.g., Josh 22:14; Judges 6:15, 27; 9:18; 11:2, 7; 16:31. Gottwald, *Tribes of Yahweh*, 285, suggested that up to five generations might have been a part of a bēt 'av. Bendor (*Social Structure*, 31) suggests that it was three or four generations.
87. Huebner, "Mediterranean Family," 12.
88. Stager "Archaeology," 19.
89. Brody, "Extended Family." See also Calloway, "Visit with Ahilud," for a village of "six clusters of houses."

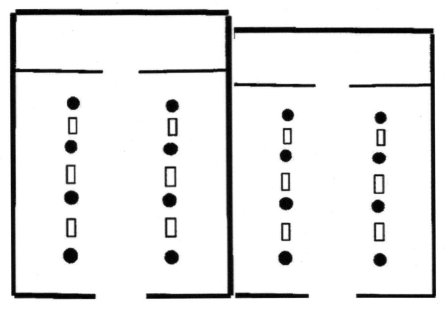

Fig. 3.7 Most Iron Age family compounds shared one or two walls. Illustration by author.

The dimensions of the houses are not usually identical but similar. They also may be a bit more asymmetrical than represented above but the overall effect is as we have presented here. The fact that these houses share a wall seems to imply a close familial relationship between the two households. Thus the inferences of Stager and Brody are sound. These compounds would be, as I understand it, family units between the *bēt 'av*, the "house(hold) of the father," and the larger unit, the *mishpaḥah*, which we will discuss below.[90] Following Faust and Bunimovitz, I regard the individual house in the rural village as representing the three-generational *bēt 'av*, the compound (when they existed) as an extension of the *bēt 'av*, and the village as the *mishpaḥah* (sometimes translated "clan"). The compound housing arrangements would be the result of the breakup of a *bēt 'av*. After the grandfather dies, the younger brother(s), if there are any, build his/their own houses next door. Each of the surviving brothers, then, becomes the grandfather of a new *bēt 'av*.

90. Stager, "Archaeology," 20–22 maintains that the compounds were the *bēt 'av*, the extended (three-generational) family, and that only five persons or so lived in each house comprising a nuclear family. His conclusions seem inaccurate in light of more recent data.

Fig. 3.8 Reconstruction of small village. Drawing by Giselle Hasel. Used by permission of Eerdmans Publishing Co. Drawing by Giselle Hasel in Dever, *Ordinary People*, 146.

The Village

Yoseph, his brother, and cousins exit their common courtyard and walk out into the center of the village. Their village has around 120 persons living in it (ten houses), most of whom are related to one another. It is comforting to know that in times of trouble your relatives and neighbors in the village will protect you and ensure your subsistence. It has also been very helpful to Yoseph, his aging father, and his brother that there is extra help in large construction projects such as building terraces, without which farming on the hillsides would be impossible. They greet their more distant cousins as they too begin to walk out of the village and into their fields. Most live huddled together in the village. Few live on an isolated farm. The farmers and the animals live in the village (in the same house) from which they go out every morning to farm their surrounding fields only to return in the evening.[91]

Dever places Iron Age settlements in Israel into four "Tiers": Tier 1 is Capital Cities; Tier 2 is Urban Centers (with over 1000 population); Tier

---

91. As Tannous, "Arab Village Community," 526, noted for the Arab villages of his day.

3 is Towns (300–1000 persons); and Tier 4 is Villages (50–300 persons).[92] He lists twelve settlements that qualify as Tier 4 villages.

Faust has surveyed fifteen villages that are about the same size as Dever's Tier 4 villages.[93] They average about 120 persons per village[94] (following Dever's guideline of 100 persons on average inhabiting one acre of village space[95]). Both Dever and Faust list the characteristics of these small villages:

Dever	Faust
1. They are small (3 to 5 acres).	1. The villages are nucleated and situated on a hilltop or hillside.
2. They are compactly organized (no street planning).	2. They are on average about one hectare in size.[97]
3. They often have a boundary wall.	3. There was a boundary wall around all of them.
4. They have no monumental architecture.	4. All houses in the villages were four-room houses.
5. They were economically self-sufficient.[96]	5. Most residential houses were 120–130m2 (1291 square feet to 1399 square feet).
	6. The villages had oil and wine production.
	7. There were no public buildings.[98]

Their descriptions then are very similar. We should imagine our hypothetical village as the artist's sketch above but with the addition of boundary walls. In a village that size, of course, everyone knows everyone else and probably everyone is related. Dever's observation that the villages were "compactly organized" reminds of the ethnological observations of Tannous with respect to the village planning of his day:

92. Dever, *Ordinary People*, 48–49.
93. Faust, *Archaeology*, 130–43.
94. See also Schloen, *House*, 155, who cites surveys in Samaria during the 1970s and 1980s. The surveys indicated that the average size of the villages was 0.5 hectares or around 1.25 acres. He therefore concludes that most villages had around 100–125 people living in them.
95. Dever, *Ordinary People*, 72. Many historians/archaeologists prefer a population density of 160–200 persons per acre. See Fiensy, "Village Life," 182, for a survey of ideas. If we accept the lower figure of 160 persons per acre, then our hypothetical village of 1.25 acres would have roughly 200 inhabitants.
96. Dever, *Ordinary People*, 84. For the self-sufficiency of the villages, see Falconer, "Village Economy," 122. Larger populations could not feed themselves and hence needed to import food.
97. But then Faust gives the size of his villages as ranging from 0.3 hectares to 1 hectare. Only one village was 1 hectare in size. The average of his 15 villages was 0.5 hectares or about 1.25 acres. See Faust, *Archaeology*, 130–43.
98. Faust, *Archaeology*, 130.

A compact, nucleated form of structure is the first striking impression one gets of the Middle Eastern village. It is a conglomeration of houses standing close to each other, divided by winding alleys and paths that do not seem to have any regular design.[99]

If the individual pillared house comprised the *bēt 'av*, the village must have been the משפחה. The *mishpaḥah*[100]—usually translated "extended family" or "clan"[101]—was a subdivision of the tribe. According to Norman Gottwald, they were groups of *batei 'av* ("houses of the father") all of whose members had mutual obligations to extend the assistance of their own *bēt 'av* to any needy *bēt 'av* within the *mishpaḥah*. If a *bēt 'av* were for some reason, for example, "decimated" the *mishpaḥah* would take the surviving members into other *batei 'av*. In general, wrote Gottwald, the *mishpaḥah* "[sustained] the family in its vulnerable autonomy."[102] Carol Meyers affirms regarding the *mishpaḥah*:

> In the prestate period, with few, if any, institutions beyond the local level to guarantee behavior and mediate conflict, the concept of "shared blood" was a critical way for securing trust and assuring willingness to engage in mutual aid.[103]

But the clan or extended family not only guaranteed subsistence, it also cooperated in large projects such as community food-processing installations (olive presses and wine presses); building large storage units; building boundary walls; and especially building terraces. The last item, terraces, was a technological innovation that enabled Iron Age Israelites to live and subsist on the very hilly terrain of Judah and Samaria. According to Faust, their construction would have required a large number of people and thus argues for a large kinship group.[104]

---

99. Tannous, "Arab Village Community," 528. For other ethnographic references to the haphazard arrangement of streets and alleys in Middle Eastern villages see: Kramer, *Village Ethnoarchaeology*, 85, 88; Lutfiyya, *Baytin*, 20; Sweet, *Tell Toqaan*, 51. These authors speak of "winding alleys"; crooked and narrow streets; and of paths in the village "twist(ing) around corners of long blocks of compounds."
100. For the various kinship units see Josh 7:14 and Judg 9:1; 18:19. See also Gottwald, *Tribes*, 291, for a good interpretation of the Judges passage.
101. W. Holladay, *Lexicon*, 221. Cf. Gottwald, *Tribes*, 301–5; C. J. H. Wright, "Family," 761.
102. Gottwald, *Tribes*, 261, 315f. Cf. D. Hopkins, *Highlands*, 257f.; C. J. H. Wright, "Family," 763. Bendor, *Social Structure*, 83–84, takes issue with Gottwald who doubted that the *mishpaḥah* was actually a biological, kinship unit.
103. Meyers, "Family," 37.
104. See Faust, "Rural Community," 24, 30.

Fig. 3.9 Terraces in Judean hill country. Photograph by the author.

There were also cooperative endeavors among the women. Carol Meyers lists two in particular: assisting in childbirth through midwifery and assisting at funerals. These activities would have often required help from outside the household/*bēt 'av* and would have perhaps formed more intimate bonds among the women than the men enjoyed in their daily activities.[105]

The clans or *mishpaḥot* were made up of patrilineal and patrilocal families.[106] In general, the entire village comprised the *mishpaḥah*.[107] These villages were probably endogamous as well.[108] Thus, everyone was related on several levels. Therefore, from the village you found a spouse for your son or daughter; you received assistance in time of need; you received cooperation in large building projects such as terraces; and you found your collectivist identity.[109]

105. C. Meyers, "Family," 38.
106. C. Meyers, "Family," 34; C. J. H. Wright, "Family," 762.
107. See Dever, *Ordinary People*, 158; C. Meyers, "Family," 37; Ebeling, *Women's Lives*, 26; C. J. H. Wright, "Family," 762; Bendor, *Social Structure*, 118.
108. C. Meyers, "Family," 36; Bendor, *Social Structure*, 84. Endogamy seems to be the preference throughout the Middle East today in rural villages. See Kramer, *Village Ethnoarchaeology*, 21; Lutfiyya, *Baytin*, 130. In the Jordanian village Lutfiyya reports on, they preferred to marry paternal cousins.
109. For collectivist identity, compare Fuller, *Buarij*, 29, who notes that in the village she studied (in

The Meal

At the end of the day, the family gathers in the house for the meal. The largest and most important meal is the last meal of the day.[110] The first two are merely "snacks" in our terminology.[111] Rachel, her sister-in-law, the concubine, and her thirteen-year-old daughter labored for hours to make the bread and then in the afternoon put on the oven a pot of lentils[112] with a few vegetables and herbs. They will also eat cheese that she had prepared some days ago and is now ready to be eaten. The family will gather in their second-floor living/dining/sleeping room, sitting on the floor around the large pot of stew placed beside the loaves of flat bread. There are no forks or spoons with which to eat. Each one scoops food with his/her (right) hand or with the flat bread.[113] The men kneel or squat around the food items and the women and older girls stand to one side waiting for the men to finish.[114] They do not eat with the men ordinarily.[115]

The entire family convenes at the end of each day in such a manner. Undoubtedly, Rachel's widowed father-in-law would eat with her nuclear family and perhaps the concubine would join them. Sometimes the entire extended family eats together. Ethnographical information would incline us toward thinking, however, that Rachel's brother-in-law and family usually ate in their own living/dining/sleeping room.

Lebanon) everyone lives in close proximity to each other. There is very little individualism and very little privacy. "They seem not to want solitude." For collectivist identity in ancient Israel see C. Meyers, *Rediscovering Eve*, 118–21.

110. King and Stager, *Life in Biblical Israel*, 67.

111. Sweet reports that in the village she studied (*Tell Toqaan*, 128), which was in Syria, they ate for breakfast tea and leftover bread (sometimes only tea); and for lunch bread, onions, and leftovers from last night's dinner.

112. נזיד See Holladay, *Lexicon*, 232. Lentils are mentioned in the Bible in the following places: Gen 25:29, 34; 2 Kgs 4:38; and Hag 2:13.

113. King and Stager, *Life in Biblical Israel*, 67.

114. Cf. ethnographically, Sweet, *Tell Toqaan*, 131; Amiry and Tamari, *Palestinian Village House*, 28.

115. King and Stager, *Life in Biblical Israel*, 67n65, suggest that the women did not eat with the men but, like Arab households they were familiar with, stood by to serve or assist and, then, after the men were finished, ate. They suggest that the women were like Abraham in the story of the three visiting angels. Abraham is said to have stood by while the angels ate (Gen 18:8–9). For ethnographic support for this practice, see Sweet, *Tell Toqaan*, 131; and the next note. C. Meyers disagrees with King and Stager on this issue and suggests (private correspondence) that segregating women from the evening meal is a later Muslim practice.

Fig. 3.10 Arab men ("farmers") eating. Notice that they sit on the floor on a mat, that they eat with their hands, and that there are no women eating with them. Used by permission of Georg Olms Verlag. In Dalman, *Haus*, photo 107. The photograph is c. 1900.

After the men finish, the women and children can eat what is left. There surely would have been bread and stew left (and meat when served but perhaps not the choicest cuts of the meat). The women clean up the cooking pot for the next day.

What did the Israelites eat? Borowski published a well-known essay on the "Mediterranean Diet" that compared the Old Testament texts with the current Bedouin and Druze practices. He concluded that Israelites in the Iron Age rarely ate meat, mostly ate fruits, vegetables, milk products (yogurt, cheese, and butter), and of course, grains (either as bread or as a porridge). When they did eat meat, only on special occasions maintained Borowski (i.e., when hosting a guest or at a festival), it was mostly mutton but perhaps some fowl.[116]

But in a recent publication, Nathan MacDonald has challenged Borowski's notion of a Mediterranean diet. Some of the items found in this diet (notably tomatoes and potatoes) were unknown to the Israelites. Even some of those items specifically referred to in the Bible were probably rarely seen by the average Israelite. The Old Testament speaks hyperbolically in describing a land flowing with milk and honey. The promises of extraordinary fertility and abundance, maintains MacDonald (e.g., Deut 8:8), are metaphorical.[117]

If we follow MacDonald, the average Israelite probably ate a very narrow range of foods. Certainly, the "Mediterranean triad" (grain, olives, grapes) was regularly on the menu. The archaeological evidence (wine presses, olive presses, and ovens for baking bread) makes it certain that these three (also well attested in the literary sources) were the mainstays of the diet. But beyond that, the options were limited to mostly pulses (beans and lentils) and milk products. The average Israelite probably never ate pomegranates or nuts. Dates would have been rather rare as well. Rather, their diet was centered on grains that supplied from 53 to 75 percent of their daily caloric intake.[118]

On the other hand, MacDonald also opines that the Israelites ate more meat than Borowski and others have allowed in their studies of the ancient diet. First, he looks at the faunal remains from various archaeological sites. Although some of these bones may have been from animals (sheep/goats and cattle) used either for milking or for pulling the plow, some of them (most?) must have been the result of slaughtering young and thus used only for meat. The numbers of these

116. Borowski, "Mediterranean Diet." Cf. King and Stager, *Life in Biblical Israel*, 68.
117. MacDonald, *Israelites Eat?* 6–8.
118. MacDonald, *Israelites Eat?* 9, 19, 23, 91.

faunal remains are too high to have been mostly used for secondary purposes (milk, wool, and pulling the plow). It appears from the ratio, observes Macdonald, that they preferred to eat the sheep or goats over the cattle.[119] MacDonald maintains that vegetables were not valued by the Israelites based on Proverbs 15:17 (a dubious conclusion).[120]

But we need more guidance in interpreting the faunal remains. Merely noting numbers of bones does not seem adequate to argue for a greater rate of meat consumption than has been thought. MacDonald has not made his case for increased meat consumption in the Iron Age.

A better argument has been mounted by Sapir-Hen, Gadot, and Finkelstein based on the age at death of the animals. Merely counting animal bones does not tell us whether the animals were used only as meat or for secondary uses (milk, wool, plowing). But these three scholars, based on the age in which the animals were slaughtered, argue that in the urban areas (Jerusalem in their study) people tended to eat more meat while in the rural villages, the residents tended to use animals more for secondary purposes. This conclusion is based on the fact that the animals in the city were younger when slaughtered and larger. The animals' remains found in the villages indicated that they tended to be both smaller (thus probably females used originally for milking) and older (slaughtered only after milk production ended) when they were slaughtered. Therefore, one could conclude that in the rural villages, they ate less meat than in the cities.[121] Borowski may have been at least *partly* correct. They evidently did not eat meat for most meals, but maybe more often than only on the rare occasions he lists.[122]

---

119. MacDonald, *Israelites Eat?*, 25. See Firmage, "Zoology (Fauna)," 1121–23, who gives a lengthy list of faunal remains from Israelite sites. For the Iron Age he lists fourteen occupation levels at eleven sites. Three of these sites have bone remains of well over 1000 pieces. But do these remains represent slaughter of the animals after being used for years for milking, for wool production, and for pulling a plow, or were most of these animals slaughtered young for their meat without any reference to secondary uses? I cannot find a reliable way to answer this question based in this data alone. But see below in the study of Sapir-Hen, Gadot, and Finkelstein, "Animal Economy."

120. MacDonald, *Israelites Eat?* 25. MacDonald has relied too much on rabbinic texts to help establish food customs in the Iron period. See pp. 35 and 43.

121. See Sapir-Hen, Gadot, and Finkelstein, "Animal Economy." These findings agree with those of Baruch Rosen at 'Izbet Ṣarṭah ("Subsistence Economy"). Rosen found that, based on the bone evidence, only 6.8 percent of the sheep/goats were butchered young. Shafer-Elliott, *Food*, 111 agrees. She studied two rural farmsteads in comparison with two houses in cities and found evidence (based on the age at death and size of the faunal remains) that the urbanites used animals mostly for meat while the rural residents used them mostly for secondary purposes. See also an examination of another bone dump in Jerusalem in Bar-Oz et al., "Holy Garbage."

122. Kramer (*Village Ethnoarchaeology*, 40–44) observed in her village that a household of six to seven persons might eat one to four sheep/goats in the winter when the animals do not produce much milk. That rate of consumption does not seem like a lot of meat-eating but perhaps is a greater consumption of meat than Borowski thought.

There have been some interesting archaeological studies on diet in the Iron Age. Of course, the caution is that these are studying one location and only one time period. They may not be indicators of the average diet. Still, they furnish us with a useful means of comparison. Let us take a look at two of these studies examining Iron II period remains. To consider the first study, from an eighth-century BCE site in Jerusalem, we need to return to our rather unpleasant sampling (in chapter 2 under "Morbidity") of a latrine or cesspit in the City of David. The reader will recall that the fecal remains from this latrine showed a high infestation of parasites. But in addition to examining for parasites, archaeobotanists (or palaeobotanists) examined them for ancient pollen. Based on the pollen remains, they discerned that the inhabitants had eaten a richly varied vegetable diet (see table below).[123]

The second sampling was from an excavation in Ashkelon and dates from the late seventh century BCE. The archaeobotanists took 138 soil samples from a building that had been burned in the conflagration caused by Nebuchadnezzar's army. The seeds in the soil had been charred and therefore preserved. The samples included 20,000 plant remains, 7000 cereal grains, 9000 fruit seeds, and 2000 weed seeds. After putting the soil samples through a flotation tank process, they found evidence that the inhabitants had eaten foods well known already from the literature (see table). Although the inhabitants were Philistines not Hebrews, the authors surmised that much of their food supply came from the Judean and Samarian hill country. Thus, the Israelites were growing (and eating) and exporting these foods.[124]

Cesspit in eighth-century BCE Jerusalem	House in seventh-century BCE Ashkelon
• Mustard family: Cabbage, mustard, radishes, turnips	• Grains: Wheat, barley
• Carrot family: Parsley, caraway, coriander, cumin, dill	• Nuts: Almonds
• Mint family: Hyssop, thyme, marjoram, sage, mint	• Fruits: Figs, grapes, pomegranates, olives
• Composite family: Lettuce, endive, artichokes, chicory	• Legumes: Chickpeas and lentils

123. Cahill et al., "It Had to Happen."
124. Weiss and Kisley, "Weeds and Seeds."

So what was on the Israelite table? Quite a variety of things according to these two studies. The caveat is that these two sites only offer a snapshot of one family's eating habits in each case. How representative are these two samples for Israel as whole in all time periods? Perhaps not very representative. These may have been rather well-to-do families and not good examples of the poor peasant's diet. Were these foods available all year long? Probably not.

A further question is how healthy was their diet. Did they have enough to eat? The answers to these questions have been debated in the last decades. Some have tried to calculate the possible daily caloric intake per person based on the arable land available to the village and other factors.[125] Those engaging in this method of answering the questions usually have concluded that the Israelites had plenty to eat; there was no malnutrition.

Baruch Rosen,[126] for example, in a detailed study, used land analysis, silo analysis in the village, and analysis of the animal bones at 'Izbet Ṣarṭah to conclude that the meat and milk available per person supplied around 350 calories per day and that the grains grown could easily have supplied the rest of the daily caloric needs. His calculations seem reasonable. The caveat is always against extrapolating one village's economic situation onto all of the highlands of Canaan.

But such calculations, although interesting, may not be the most reliable method for determining malnutrition. Another way is to examine the skeletal remains for evidence of nutritional challenges. One such study was done on a Jerusalem tomb containing sixty individuals and dating to the seventh century BCE. The pathological results showed that almost one in three (31.5 percent) suffered from a condition called cribra orbitalia (or porotic hyperostosis), which is spongy tissue in the cranial vault. This condition is usually attributed to malnutrition (iron or protein deficiency) and/or parasitism that causes anemia and general weakness in the sufferer.[127] The lesions are usually attributed to a high cereal diet, which lends itself to such deficiencies. Hence, physical anthropologists in the past have presumed malnutrition (not necessarily a lack of food but a lack of the right kinds of food) as the cause of cribra orbitalia. One might eat sufficient quantities of calories daily but not the correct balance providing protein, vitamins, and minerals.

125. See MacDonald's survey in *Israelites Eat?*, 45–57.
126. Rosen, "Subsistence Economy."
127. MacDonald, *Israelites Eat?*, 82; Scheidel, *Death on the Nile*, 138–39.

One should balance any conclusions about cribra orbitalia with wider evidence, however. This condition is very commonly seen in skeletal remains, not only in Israel in all periods[128] but also widely in the Middle East and the Mediterranean world.[129] Its presence in the skulls of the individuals buried in Jerusalem from the Iron Age is not remarkable. Was everyone undernourished until modern times? Possibly, but if so, it tells us nothing about conditions in ancient Israel relative to her neighbors.

Second, today, this association of cribra orbitalia and iron deficiency is being debated.[130] Pathologists are not as certain as they once were as to the causes of this ubiquitous condition in premodern human beings. There does seem to be a correlation between high rates of cribra orbitalia and high child mortality.[131] Still, the evidence from the Jerusalem tomb is not conclusive to establish that some persons in the seventh century were nutritionally challenged. The truth is that we have no way of determining at present whether there was enough food (or enough of the right kinds of food) to maintain good health.

Finally, MacDonald suggests, based on a study of the skeletal remains of Tel Qiri (Persian period) in the Jezreel valley that women may have been underfed, at least in terms of the available meat. The women in this village were unusually shorter than the men. The physical anthropologist who examined the human skeletal remains suggested that the men ate the butchered meat and the women did not. MacDonald seems inclined to accept this interpretation and to suggest that it applied also throughout the Iron Age but does caution us that the sample size was only five males and three females.[132] In my opinion, such a small sample size should be discarded. Even were the sample size a bit larger, it would not prove that the women were smaller because of the preferential feeding of males. There is thus no hard evidence that the women and girls were deprived of nutrition in favor of the men.[133]

---

128. See Mitchell, "Palaeopathology of Skulls"; Mitchell, "Child's Health"; and Smith, Bornemann, and Zias, "Skeletal Remains."
129. See the table in Mitchell, "Child's Health," 40, which lists five sites outside of Israel. Also see Scheidel, *Death on the Nile*, 138–40, who cites two detailed studies from Egypt. See also Piontek and Kozlowsk, "Frequency"; Facchini, Rastelli, and Brasili, "Cribra Orbitalia"; and Keenleyside and Panayotova, "Cribra Orbitalia"; for studies from Poland in the Middle Ages, and Italy and the Black Sea area in antiquity.
130. See Walker et al., "Causes of Porotic Hyperostosis."
131. Scheidel, *Death on the Nile*, 140.
132. MacDonald, *Israelites Eat?*, 87. For an argument similar to MacDonald's (with respect to the Second Temple period), see Ilan, *Integrating*, 205, who surmised that girls were underfed and sometimes died of starvation. Her conclusions, like MacDonald's, are based on inadequate data. See also Wells, "Obstetric Hazards," for a similar argument relevant to classical Greece.
133. One can understand MacDonald's sensitivity to this culture. Canaan reports a saying current

It is now dark; the meal has been eaten; the cleanup is finished. The family stays up a bit longer to tell stories about the glories of their people in the past. Finally, it is bedtime and Rachel can, mercifully, rest.

Applications for the Study of the Hebrew Bible

Our study of the Israelite household does not have the kind of implications that finding the Shishak inscription, the relief sculptures of Sennacherib, or the Solomonic gates of Gezer had. It does, however, carry with it the ability to reconstruct the background of several texts and of the Hebrew Bible in general. To these smaller implications we now turn:

1. Our study of the Israelite household makes certain texts clearer. We can understand how the ancient readers of the stories would have experienced them. It is easier to imagine the story. We can, for example, consider the story of Jephthah's rash vow and its tragic consequences more intelligently. He presumed the first thing out of his house would be one of the livestock being housed in it and not his daughter (Judg 11:31). Likewise one can appreciate Job's utter devastation when all of his children (and grandchildren?) were killed while they feasted in his oldest son's house (who had become his own "father of a house," Job 1:18–19). Job and his wife lost their entire support group in a day. Their extended family, through which their collectivist personality was expressed, vanished.

2. Second, the conditions for women in Iron Age Israel appear rather bleak. All persons in those days had short life spans, but women were especially at risk. This situation gives one pause in reading Proverbs 31:10–31. This remarkable (model) wife can, it appears, do anything—except live a long life. Anyone who works like that will not live a long time. The risks of childbearing alongside the

among the Palestinian Arabs of his day: "nothing will make men happy (lucky) except their (male) children" (Canaan, *Arab House*, 27). When one considers such a culture—which may also have been the culture of the Bible in its valuation of women—one has little trouble imagining females eating after the males have eaten. But such a possibility certainly does not mean that females were fed less or sometimes not fed at all. (See Garroway, *Children*, 128, and Exod 21:10 for a prohibition of reducing a female slave's food.) To be more cautious, perhaps one could surmise *at most* not that they were deprived of the meat (or food) entirely but may have been deprived of the best cuts of meat. In such an understanding the choicest parts would go to the grandfather, the second best went to his oldest son, and so forth. In this scenario, the women ate last but certainly still ate. The reader should remember that when a lamb was butchered, it had to be eaten within a day since otherwise the meat would spoil. They needed everyone in the family to join in the feast.

daily grind of work took its toll. Could one reason that more women are not featured in the Hebrew Bible simply be because not enough of them lived long enough to become famous?

3. Indications are that the Israelites mostly had enough food (if not always the right nutrition) to avoid starvation. The exception was the occasional famine year, of course. But the archaeological evidence does not support a general caloric deficiency. The *bēt 'av* functioned effectively in normal years to protect the needs of all its members.

4. The existence of the *bēt 'av* meant that no one was left alone. All had a support group in times of loss and tragedy. There were no loners in this culture. They all lived huddled together (along with their livestock!) in their extended family houses. The abandoned beggars so commonly seen in the New Testament world of Palestine must have been very rare in Iron Age Israel. The words of Psalm 133:1 seem especially apt for the *bēt 'av*: "How good and how pleasant it is when siblings dwell (closely) together!"

4

It Is Lived So Briefly: Osteoarchaeology and the New Testament

I often tell my students, "A good historian is just a very nosey person." By that I mean that a historian wants to know everything about the people of the past. As I indicated in the last chapter, the late twentieth century saw a transformation in the writing of history. No longer were historians only interested in the great men and women, the great battles, and the great nations of the past. They did not simply ask about the emperors, the generals, and the monuments. They began to ask what life was like for the ordinary men and women. What did they do for a living? What did they eat? How did they treat each other? Where did they live? What diseases did they suffer from? How long did they live? What did they think about certain issues? Was their life a misery? What would an ordinary day be like?

In this quest, historians have sought windows into the past in order to understand daily life.[1] They are like security guards who watch people through their security cameras. Sometimes the camera is a papyrus text that describes the family situation of the person composing the document. For example, a text from Egypt dated to 13 BCE records

---

1. See e.g. Hezser, ed., *Oxford Handbook*; Dever, *Ordinary People*; King and Stager, *Life in Biblical Israel*; Borowski, *Daily Life*; Nakhai, "Embracing the Domestic"; Magness, *Stone and Dung*.

a marriage agreement between bride and groom. The bride brings with her a dowry of two gold earrings and some silver drachmae and promises to fulfill her duties. The husband promises to treat the bride well and to provide for her; otherwise he must forfeit the dowry.[2] With this one text we get a brief look into the family situation of a young couple entering into legal marriage, presumably with all the hope and joy that newly married couples have experienced since time immemorial. But in case it does not work out, the family has protected their daughter with the dowry.

Sometimes the camera is a public building such as a synagogue. The newly discovered synagogue at Magdala on the western shore of the Sea of Galilee in Israel is an example. The viewer can, upon viewing the site, picture the worshipers seated on the benches that ring the walls of the structure. One can imagine the synagogue leader standing behind the stone table that evidently held a stand on which the Torah scroll lay for reading. The visitor to the site can almost hear the voices of those gathered for prayer and study from 2000 years ago.[3]

Or the camera can be a collection of inscriptions (graffiti) from the walls of brothels and even of ordinary houses in which men boast of their sexual exploits and indicate their view of women. They demonstrate the ancient Roman view of machismo, of the control and dominance of females.[4] These few sentences tell us much about—give us a window into—the Roman attitudes of sexuality and maleness.

Historians use whatever means are available—written texts such as the papyri and inscriptions, but also archaeological ruins—to re-create the lives of ancient folk. The same interest is present in New Testament studies. New Testament interpreters now ask about the sort of people who would have listened to Jesus teach and who would have read the New Testament. What did these folk do for a living? What was it like to walk around in their skin? How would they have heard the New Testament?

As a result of asking questions about the ordinary folk, biblical scholars began to use methods and insights from sociology, cultural anthropology, and economics. From the pioneers in this field[5] up to and

---

2. See the texts in C. K. Barrett, *New Testament Background*, 40.
3. See Stefano De Luca and Anna Lena, "Magdala, Taricheae," and Lee Levine, "Synagogues."
4. See John Dominic Crossan and Jonathan L. Reed, *In Search of Paul*, 262.
5. See, among others, Gerd Theissen, *Sociology of Early Palestinian Christianity*; Howard Clark Kee, *Christian Origins in Sociological Perspective*; Bruce Malina, *The New Testament World*; Robert R. Wilson, *Sociological Approaches to the Old Testament*; and Bernhard Lang, ed., *Anthropological Approaches to the Old Testament*.

including its more recent exponents,[6] the goal has been to put a face on the characters of the Hebrew Bible and the New Testament. Scholars ask what it must have been like to live in the world of Palestine/Israel, in the Ancient Near East, or in the Greco-Roman world. What were their values and their perceptions and how might knowing the answers to these questions help in understanding the biblical text of the Hebrew Bible or the New Testament? The rise of the social sciences in biblical interpretation was the result of a perceived need for a "sociological imagination" to understand the scenes and scenarios of scripture.[7] These interpreters maintain that merely collecting information is not enough to facilitate interpretation of the Hebrew Bible and New Testament; one must have the means of "envisioning, investigating, and understanding the interrelation of texts and social contexts. . . ."[8] The goal of the social science movement in interpretation has been to enable the interpreter to get to know the people for whom the texts were originally written.

New Testament scholars have also turned repeatedly to the discoveries in archaeology. And in recent years, even archaeologists of Israel and the Greco-Roman world have begun to change their focus. Now they not only study the architectural features of the cities and the great monuments of antiquity. They also look at the diet and morbidity of the ancient folk by examining really odd things, such as the remains of ancient rubbish heaps and latrines (see chapter 2).[9] As we noted in chapters 2 and 3, archaeoparasitologists can determine that a large number of the people suffered from intestinal parasites since their eggs show up in the remains of the latrines. The historian can then conclude that many of the ancients experienced ill health due to a simple lack of nutrition.

Historians have also turned to an examination of the human skeletal remains. The skeletal remains are about as personal as we are ever going to get for the investigation of ancient persons. This is so because the common people, in the main, wrote nothing. (For that matter, most

---

6. Douglas Oakman, *Jesus and the Peasants*; Ekkehard W. Stegemann and Wolfgang Stegemann, *The Jesus Movement*; Anthony J. Blasi, Jean Duhaime, and Paul-André Turcotte, eds., *Handbook of Early Christianity*; Dietmar Neufeld and Richard E. Demaris, eds., *Understanding the Social World of the New Testament*; John H. Elliott, *What Is Social-Scientific Criticism?*; C. Osiek, *What Are They Saying About the Social Setting of the New Testament?*; R. L. Rohrbaugh, ed., *The Social Sciences and New Testament Interpretation*; and J. H. Neyrey and E. C. Stewart, eds., *The Social World of the New Testament*.
7. See John Elliott, *Social-Scientific Criticism*, 13.
8. Ibid.
9. Harter, Mumcuoglu, and Zias, "Toilet Practices"; Mitchell and Tepper, "Intestinal Parasitic Worm Eggs"; Edward Neufeld, "Hygiene Conditions"; Zias, "Death and Disease"; Cahill et al., "It Had to Happen." See chapter 2 of this volume.

of the elites wrote nothing.) Thus we cannot read their literary works; we cannot even read their (nonliterary) diaries. But they did leave some of themselves behind: their physical remains.

We can meet these people in their skeletal remains and learn a great deal about the kind of lives they lived. We can find out: how tall they were, if they suffered from chronic illnesses, how long they lived,[10] if they were well nourished, to what ethnic group they belonged, whether they died of natural causes or violently, genetic affinities, the state of bodily development, wear and tear from labor, and social conditions.[11] The bones tell us many things.

The modern study of paleodemography through osteoarchaeology (or bone archaeology) began with the publications of J. Lawrence Angel,[12] who in 1947 collected 384 skeletal remains from Greece covering the Neolithic through the Byzantine eras. Although the sample size for each era was small, he nonetheless produced some very interesting and innovative results for his time. The rates of infant mortality and life expectancy rose and declined a bit as the eras changed, but over all there was a very high rate of infant mortality and a very short life expectancy for adults.

Publications of analyses of skeletal remains from the Second Temple period in Israel began in the 1960s.[13] Although the gathering, analysis, and publication of skeletal remains is a large problem in Israel because of religious opposition,[14] there has been a rather steady issue of such reports as more and more intact tombs have been discovered. There is now—as the reader will see below—quite a large database of osteological information out there. At times, the bones are not very well preserved and so only the most basic information can be gleaned. At other times, the anthropologists seem to have been able to be quite precise in the age at death and general health of the individual.

10. Grmek, *Diseases*, 383n40: "The determination of age at death from these skeletal remains is based on tooth eruption, formation of long bones, cranial suture closure, metamorphosis of the pubic symphysis, radiographic translucency of proximal femur and humerus, dental wear, and a variety of minor indicators."
11. Patricia Smith, "Skeletal Analysis"; Eakins, "Human Osteology and Archeology"; and Grmek, *Diseases*, 51. See also Nagar and Sonntag, "Byzantine Period Burials"; and Steckoll, "Preliminary Excavation Report."
12. Angel, "Length of Life."
13. See among the first: Nathan, "Skeletal Remains from Naḥal Ḥever."
14. See C. Meyers, "Archaeology," 76.

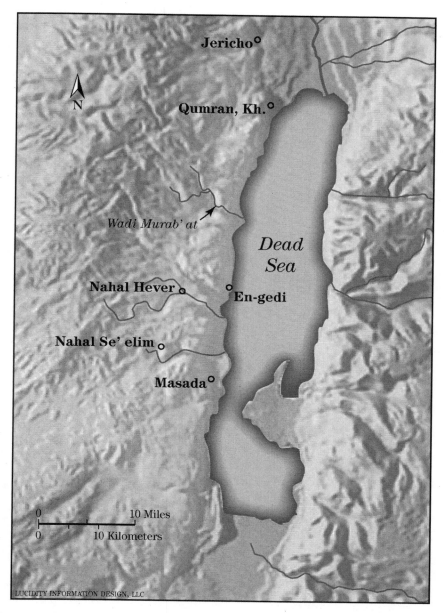

Fig. 4.1 Map showing Jericho, Qumran, En-gedi, and Naḥal Ḥever where skeletal remains in tombs were removed and studied. Map by Lucidity.

I propose, in this chapter, to survey reports of burial remains to get a clearer picture of the people of Palestine/Israel in the late Second

103

Temple period. There really is a surprising number of skeletal analyses published (most from thirty or forty years ago). We can collect these studies and assemble an acceptable sample size to draw demographic conclusions.

The sites we will survey include[15] ten tombs or tomb complexes in Jerusalem; one in Galilee; four sites (eight tombs) in Judea and southern Samaria; and four sites on the western shores of the Dead Sea including Jericho (130 tombs); cave 8 from Naḥal Ḥever; nine tombs at En-Gedi; and several collections[16] of the skeletal remains from the Qumran cemetery. The ten tombs/tomb complexes in Jerusalem are: Giv'at ha-Mivtar, Mt. Scopus (twice), French Hill (both LH and ER tombs), the Caiaphas tomb, the Akeldama tombs, the Arnona tomb, the Abba cave, and an unpublished tomb described in a report on Jericho.[17]

We will work from a total database of 1475 individuals. Of course, not every individual in the tombs can be factored into a given question since often the remains are too disintegrated to indicate more than a very rough age (not a precise age and not gender). To answer one query, we need only to know if the individual died in youth (before age twenty; Table E). Virtually all of the skeletal remains (though not all even for this general question) can be used to formulate an answer to this investigation. But for other calculations (such as life expectancy by sex at adulthood, Table H) we need a fairly accurate estimate of the age at death and a determination of the sex of the individual. Therefore, Table H will have the smallest sample size.

How does our total database of 1475 compare with that of other demographers studying the ancient world? Bagnall and Frier had 1084 persons in their database. Russell had 813 persons in his Egyptian database, 2345 persons from Asia, Greece, and Illyricum, and 1111 (males only) from Iberia.[18] Our sample size of evidence, then, is within their range.

To be sure, there are possible pitfalls in appealing to osteoarchaeology as one's main evidence. Walter Scheidel[19] lists two problems with this sort of evidence: First, he maintains that determining the precise

---

15. Compare to Tal Ilan's list of skeletal remains in *Integrating Women*, 214.
16. For Qumran see Steckoll, "Preliminary Excavation Report"; Broshi and Eshel, "Whose Bones?"; Röhrer-Ertl, "Facts and Results"; and Sheridan, "French Collection." Other reports (not useful for this study) of the skeletal remains at Qumran are: De Vaux, *Archaeology*; Bartlett, "Archaeology of Qumran"; and Bar-Adon, "Another Settlement."
17. Hachlili and Smith, "Goliath," 69.
18. See Frier, "Pannonian Evidence," 335–36. On the other hand, Wells ("Ancient Obstetric," 1235) reports a study done in 1959 using 24,848 epitaphs.
19. Scheidel, "Population and Demography," 3.

age of adult bones is difficult. Thus precision in establishing longevity models would be impossible.[20] Second, the skeletal remains might be skewed evidence since they might only witness to certain burial customs and might not inform us about migration. This is a valid caution. I would even add to it that the bones we find in tombs in Israel might belong to individuals that were somewhat elevated economically from the rest of the population. Less prosperous individuals might have been buried in shaft/cyst graves instead of more costly tombs.[21] Thus, I recognize that there are difficulties but the evidence must, in my opinion, be considered. One can't simply ignore an area of evidence because there may be difficulties in using it.

Of course, the removal, examination, and publication of information about human skeletal remains is especially difficult in Israel. First, one must find a tomb that has not been already robbed and looted. Next, the bones in the tomb must be in good enough shape to be reliably analyzed; some are not. Finally, and most challengingly, the anthropologists must be allowed to study the bones. Because of religious conflicts, this is not always permitted, especially recently.[22] Nor is this issue a problem only in Israel. Other cultures wrestle as well with the conflict between respect for the bones of the ancestors and the desires of historical investigation.[23]

Nonetheless, it appears to me that osteoarchaeology is here to stay and that it will yield many exciting and interesting results in the future. There has been since 1991 a journal devoted exclusively to publishing its findings[24] and some universities offer master's degrees in this field (e.g., the University of Edinburgh). The skeletal remains are an important line of evidence in the study of ancient demography.

Furthermore, demographers have noted that the other methods of studying populations, especially mortality, in the ancient world—tomb inscriptions, Ulpian's Life Table, and Egyptian census records pre-

---

20. Scheidel, *Death on the Nile*, 122; and ibid., "Population and Demography." Grmek, *Diseases*, 99, disagrees with this conclusion.
21. See C. Meyers, "Archaeology," 76, for the same caution with regard to Iron Age tombs. Did it require some means to own a family tomb in the Second Temple period? The answer is debated. Magness (*Stone and Dung*, 156) answers "yes." Gibson (*Final Days*, 159–61) answers "no." Gibson believes that even the poor could afford a tomb, probably one excavated by the family itself.
22. See e.g. Judy Siegel-Itzkovich, "Orthodox Jews Demand University Bury Its Bones," *British Medical Journal* (May 5, 2001). Online at http://www.bmj.com/content/322/7294/1084.5?tab=responses. See also C. Meyers, "Archaeology," 76.
23. See e.g. Ryan M. Seidemann, "Bones of Contention: A Comparative Examination of Law Governing Human Remains from Archaeological Contexts in Formerly Colonial Countries," *Louisiana Law Review* 64 (2004): 545–88.
24. *The International Journal of Osteoarchaeology.*

served on papyrus—also have their problems. For example, people were in the habit of giving out false age-related information on tombstones and especially on tax documents. There are no problem-free demographic data.[25] Thus, we need the osteological data from Palestine/Israel to supplement other evidence from the Greco-Roman environment. As classicist Tim Parkin observes, "A skeleton cannot lie about its age."[26] Further, for Palestine/Israel there really is very little demographic evidence except the osteological.

Moreover, one can offer a check or confirmation of the osteological evidence from Israel by comparing it with the evidence of the papyri, tombstone inscriptions, and even skeletal remains from elsewhere in the Roman Empire. We will see that the data from the tombs of Israel from the late Second Temple period (LH and ER) are similar to those obtained by the other means indicated above from elsewhere in the empire.

Let us begin with a very brief indication of stature and then we will turn to our main discussion of mortality. Other important and interesting issues that one could pursue with the osteoarchaeological data would be those topics mentioned just above.

Stature

One easily answered question is how tall, on average, these people were. To find an average, we will simply note the average stature of individuals (male and female) from various tombs and then average these together. Our database is difficult to assess (300–500). The reason is because some reports only give an average stature for the entire tomb complex or complexes and note that many of the individuals' remains were not measurable. Thus, the number of individuals they used to calculate their average is unknown. Nevertheless, one can gain

---

25. The following are some of the cautions offered by paleodemographers: Some of the tomb inscriptions seem to exaggerate the age of the deceased, especially the age of an older person (Russell, *Late Ancient*, 23–24). Some of the census records exaggerate the age of maternity and paternity (Bagnall and Frier, *Demography*, 42). Some of them may want a middle-aged woman to appear younger and so subtract ten years or so from her age at death. Children do not usually even get a tombstone (Durand, "Mortality Estimates," 369–70). Further, the census documents from Egypt may give incorrect data because they want to hide those men turning fourteen years to save tax money and likewise to exaggerate those in their fifties as being over sixty (Scheidel, *Death on the Nile*, 151, 156–57).

26. Parkin, *Demography*, 43. See also K. K. Éry, "Investigations": "The acquiring of factual knowledge concerning mortality conditions in the Roman era is to be expected therefore only from the demographic elaboration of the skeletal remains excavated from the cemeteries" (62).

some perspective on this question by looking at the averages submitted by these anthropologists. The table below has the results:

Table A: Stature in the ER Period in Israel[27]

Site	Male Average Height	Female Average Height
Giv' at ha-Mivtar	165.5 cm	157 cm
Meiron	165.5	148
En-Gedi	166.9	150.8
8 tombs/Judea/Samaria	166	147
Mt. Scopus	166	149
N. Ḥever	162	154
French Hill (LH)	167	146
Average[28]	165.5 (5'5")	150 (4'11")

Thus the average male in this period living in Israel/Palestine was around five feet five inches tall and the average female was four feet eleven inches tall. The men and women of Palestine/Israel were a bit smaller than those attested for Greece in the Hellenistic period. Grmek gives the averages for the Greeks at 171.8 cm for men (5'7") and 156.6 cm for women (5'1").[29]

Missing from these calculations, however, are the outlying data from a family buried in Tomb H in Jericho, sometimes called the "Goliath Family Tomb." As the name indicates, some of these persons were unusually tall in comparison with the others from their period. While we do not know exactly which ossuary belonged to the man nicknamed Goliath, the anthropologists surmise that one man in this three-generational family tomb measuring 188.5 cm (6'2"), was the one given this moniker.[30] We might compare "Goliath" at Jericho with a man 202 cm tall (6'7") found just north of Rome (from the third century CE).[31] The

---

27. The table is composed from information in: Zias, "Mount Scopus (Meiron, En-Gedi, and Mount Scopus)"; Haas, "Anthropological Observations (Giv'at ha-Mivtar)"; Nagar and Torgeé, "Biological Characteristics (8 tombs in Judea)"; Nathan, "Naḥal Ḥever"; and Arensburg and Rak, "Skeletal Remains (French Hill)."
28. This figure agrees essentially with Joe Zias, "Appendix A: Anthropological Observations," 125, who affirms that the average height of males from the Hellenistic to the Roman-Byzantine periods was 166 cm and of females was 148 cm.
29. Grmek, Diseases, 109. Gallant, Risk, 69, offers the average stature for classical Greece: 169.8 for men and 156.3 for women, about the same as the Hellenistic age.
30. Hachlili and Smith, "Genealogy of the Goliath Family," 68.
31. Minozzi et al., "Roman Giant"; and Dell'Amore, "Roman Giant."

anthropologists examining the Roman giant considered him abnormal and suffering from an endocrine disease. Thus persons well over six feet tall were quite unusual in the ancient Mediterranean and Middle Eastern world.

The scale below compares this average with averages elsewhere in the world today. The smallest persons are the inhabitants of Bolivia and the tallest are the Danes.[32]

Table B: Scale of comparison (Men)

Bolivia	Israel (Antiquity)	U.S.	Denmark
160 cm	165.5 cm	176.3 cm	182.6 cm

Table C: Scale of comparison (Women)

Bolivia	Israel (Antiquity)	U.S.	Denmark
142.2 cm	150 cm	163.1 cm	168.7 cm

Knowing about the average stature in Israel at our time period helps us to imagine the story. We are accustomed to thinking about the New Testament characters as looking like Europeans. The Hebrew Bible (1 Sam 9:2) says that Saul was head and shoulders taller than the other Israelite men. We imagine him as six and one half feet or more. The text also says the giant Goliath was six cubits and a span (or allegedly around 9 feet[33]). All of this leaves the impression that most Israelite men must have been around six feet tall with Saul a bit taller and "giants" abnormally tall. Thus, we also assume that Jesus and the disciples were the same (perhaps Jesus was like Saul).

But the skeletal remains of many Jewish men from the late Second Temple period argue otherwise. Jesus and the disciples did not look like our action heroes of today. They were not buff and did not tower over other persons (probably). Rather, they looked like most Middle Easterners look now. Jesus was probably around five feet five inches tall. These results are not earth-shaking and do not really change anyone's interpretation of specific New Testament texts but they help us place

---

32. "Human Height," *Wikipedia*. Online: https://en.wikipedia.org/wiki/Human_height. Accessed Nov. 16, 2015.
33. According to most Masoretic manuscripts. But LXX (Codex Vaticanus) reads 4½ cubits (6½ feet); LXX (other mss) read 5½ cubits (8¼ feet); and 4QSam[a] reads 4½ cubits (6½ feet). See Martin Abegg Jr., Peter Flint, and Eugene Ulrich, *The Dead Sea Scrolls Bible*, 229.

those texts into the lives of real people. We can imagine the story more realistically.

Mortality

What percentage of children died before reaching adulthood (youth mortality rate)? What was the average life span (from birth and from adulthood)? These are the kinds of questions demographers studying mortality ask. To do this study, of course, one needs the estimation of both age and sex. Unfortunately, in some cases, this calculation is simply not possible due to the poorly preserved bones.[34] But we will take the data we have, analyze it, and then compare it with the other demographic methods cited above.

We will examine four considerations. We will look at child mortality (ages 0 to five years), youth mortality (0 to nineteen years), average life span from birth, and average life span from adulthood.[35]

Let us say from the start that the study of demography has been going on among ancient historians and classicists for the last thirty or forty years. They have usually turned to the tombstone inscriptions for their information (with some profit also in searching the Egyptian papyri). They seem to agree on three observations:[36]

1. Infant mortality was shockingly high by today's standards.[37]
2. Even if one should reach the age of twenty, the life expectancy was still pretty low (somewhere in the mid-thirties to early forties).[38]
3. There was a significant gap in the life expectancy of women and men.[39]

We will see if our findings agree or disagree with these earlier observations for the Greco-Roman world in general.

Child Mortality

One of the most telling statistics in any society is its child mortality

34. For the accuracy in such determinations, see Smith, "Skeletal Analysis," 52–53.
35. For information on how anthropologists estimate age, see Brothwell, *Digging Up Bones*, 57–66; and Grmek, *Diseases*, 383n40.
36. Parkin, *Demography*, 92; Burn, "Hic breve vivitur," 10; Grmek, *Diseases*, 104.
37. See e.g. Grmek, *Diseases*, 100; Parkin, *Demography*, 92–93.
38. See Grmek, *Diseases*, 106; Bagnall and Frier, *Demography*, 109.
39. See Grmek, *Diseases*, 100; Wells, "Ancient Obstetric."

rate. This data can be a good predictor of the prosperity of a society. If the child mortality (in our case, ages 0 to five[40]) is unusually higher than the surrounding societies, then chances are that Israel in the ER period was economically deprived relative to the surrounding regions. To figure child mortality, we will divide the total number of persons identified by the anthropologists as age 0 to five years at death by the total number of individuals in the tombs. The following table presents the evidence:

Table D: Child Mortality in LH and ER Israel[41]

Tomb(s)	Number of Individuals	Number of infants (0–5)
Jericho (Goliath, tomb H)	31	10
French Hill (ER)	64	10
French Hill (LH)	33	9
Meiron	197	70
Judea/Samaria (8 tombs)	227	54 (0–9)
Caiaphas	63	26
Giv'at ha-Mivtar	35	9
Arnona	41	14
Mt. Scopus	88	34
Har Haẓofim Observatory	147	54
Akeldama	115	45
Abba	4	1
Naḥal Ḥever	19	4
En-Gedi	164	49
Totals	1228[42]	389

AVERAGE CHILD MORTALITY = 31 percent

---

40. The nomenclature changes from demographer to demographer. Usually infant mortality is measured on the basis of 0 to one year. The age at death for most skeletal remains of individuals from over two thousand years ago usually cannot be calculated that precisely. Thus, most physical anthropologists date within five years. We will use the term "child mortality" to designate those dying before age five and "youth mortality" to designate those dying before age twenty.

41. The table is produced by combined evidence in: Arieli, "Har Haẓofim Observatory"; Hachlili and Smith, "Goliath Family"; Arensburg and Rak, "French Hill"; Haas, "Anthropological Observations" (Giv'at, ha-Mivtar); Nagar and Torgeé, "Biological Characteristics" (8 tombs); Smith, Bornemann, and Zias, "Skeletal Remains" (Meiron); Zias, "Caiaphas' Tomb"; ibid., "Mount Scopus"; ibid., "Anthropological Analysis" (Akeldama); ibid., "Human Skeletal Remains" (Arnona); Nathan, "Naḥal Ḥever"; Arensburg and Belfer-Cohen, "En-Gedi"; Smith, "Abba Cave"; and Hadas, "En-Gedi."

The table is a bit problematic because one of the sources only gives data for children from 0 to nine years instead of 0 to five years as in all of the others. Still, this figure conforms rather well to other findings in other parts of the Mediterranean world. The average percentage results in a 31 percent child mortality rate for Israel in the (mostly) ER period.[43] The percentage is about seven points lower than that of contemporary Greece (38 percent).[44] Thus, based on child mortality alone—although shockingly high by modern standards—one would not conclude that Palestine/Israel was worse economically than Greece in the ER period.

But, although this child mortality rate is very high by our modern standards, it is not much different from what we can find recorded in recent, premodern history. Although child mortality (0 to five years old) is usually lower than 1 percent in wealthy countries today, in premodern times it ranged from 30 to 50 percent. In late nineteenth-century Germany as well as in India, Yemen, and Korea in 1800, the child mortality rate was over 50 percent. The healthiest countries had a rate of 30 percent. In 1800 the global average was 43 percent. (Now it is 3.4 percent.) Thus this child mortality rate for ancient Palestine/Israel is not high by premodern standards. It was toward the lower end of the range.[45]

Youth Mortality

Next we look at youth mortality. Here we want to know how many died before reaching adulthood (which we will define as age twenty). Tal Ilan,[46] from her database of 403 individuals, found a youth mortality rate of 44 percent. She wondered at the time if further results might move the number higher. Now, based on my much larger database, that question can be answered.

We will look at a sample size of 1475 individuals to determine how

---

42. Not all of the individuals in the total database can be used for this measure since the anthropologists could not always give a precise age for the children. Thus, if they only indicated that the skeletal remains were of a pre-adult or youth, we could use the data in the next table but not for calculating child mortality for which we need an age range of from 0 to five years.

43. One of the French Hill tombs is Late Hellenistic, as are the nine tombs at En-Gedi (see Hadas, "Nine Tombs"). The cemetery at Meiron dates from the first century BCE to the third century CE. Some of the tombs excavated by Nagar and Torgeé dated from the Late Hellenistic period; and finally, the remains from Cave 8 at Naḥal Ḥever are from the early second century CE.

44. Hachlili, "Goliath."

45. See Roser, "Child Mortality." Roser writes that the three most lethal diseases for children in this age range were pneumonia, diarrhea, and malaria in that order.

46. Ilan, *Integrating*, 201, 214.

many of them died before their twentieth birthday, calculating the same way we did to arrive at infant mortality. Table E has the results:

Table E: Youth Mortality in Ancient Israel (LH and ER): Data[47]

Tombs	Total Individuals	Youths (0–19)
Jericho	185 (130 tombs)	54
French Hill ER	64	19
French Hill LH	33	9
Jerusalem (Unpublished)	65	28
Meiron	197	95
8 tombs in Judea/Samaria	227	73
Caiaphas	63	43
Giv' at ha-Mivtar	35	16
Arnona	41	21
Mt. Scopus	88	42
Har Haẓofim Observatory	147	81
Akeldama	115	55
Abba Cave	4	2
Naḥal Ḥever	19	12
Qumran	28	5
En-Gedi	164	77
TOTAL	1475	632

AVERAGE YOUTH MORTALITY: 43 percent

These results are almost exactly what Ilan found using a much smaller sample size. Further, we note the following observations: First, the Caiaphas tomb is unusually high in child mortality (68 percent). This family, presumably somewhat well-to-do, or at least of middling means

47. Compiled from data in Arieli, "Har Haẓofim Observatory"; Arensburg and Smith, "Anthropological Tables"; Smith and Zias, "French Hill"; Arensburg and Rak, "French Hill"; Hachlili and Smith, "Goliath Family"; Smith, Bornemann, and Zias, "Skeletal Remains (Meiron)"; Nagar and Torgeé, "Biological Characteristics" (eight tombs); Zias, "Caiaphas"; Haas, "Giv'at ha-Mivtar"; Zias, "Arnona"; Zias, "Mount Scopus"; Zias, "Anthropological Analysis (Akeldama)"; Nathan, "Naḥal Hever"; Steckoll, "Preliminary Excavation Report"; Broshi and Eshel, "Whose Bones?"; Röhrer-Ertl, "Facts and Results."

to be able to afford a tomb,[48] must have had a genetic tendency for youth mortality since we would assume that lack of nutrition would not have been the problem. On the other hand, the Jericho (29 percent) and French Hill LH (27 percent) cemeteries exhibit very low youth mortality for this period.

These outlying figures are even more striking when we compare them with those from Athens and Olynthus in the classical period and with Rome, the Italian countryside, and the eastern Mediterranean world in the Roman imperial period:

Table F: Youth Mortality in the Greco-Roman World

Location	Youth Mortality percentage
Athens (classical)[49]	49%
Olynthus (classical)[50]	49%
Rome (imperial)[51]	54%
Italian countryside (imperial period)[52]	42%
Eastern Mediterranean (imperial period)[53]	47%

If we can assume that the cities of Athens and Rome were about average with respect to child mortality for the cities of the empire, we see how unusually high the Caiaphas tomb is and how incredibly low the two other above-mentioned tombs are. Over all, the tombs of Late Hellenistic and Early Roman Israel exhibit a youth mortality rate that is 6 percent lower than Greece, 11 percent lower than that of the city of Rome, but about the same as that evidenced from other sites in Italy. How one explains this difference (the ritual washing of Judaism, simply better DNA, better nutrition, or the lack of sanitation in the cities) remains unclear. At any rate, one had a slightly better chance of growing to adulthood in Israel than in Athens or in Rome.

Meir Bar-Ilan[54] has arrived at a similar figure for Talmudic-era Israel by using two methods: references in the rabbinic literature (especially

---

48. It is disputed as to whether this is the Caiaphas of the New Testament, the High Priest who condemned Jesus to death. See Craig A. Evans, "Excavating Caiaphas."
49. Reported in Hachlili, "Goliath."
50. Demand, *Birth*, 193n117.
51. Hopkins, "Age Structure." Hopkins's figure for Rome was based on 8065 inscriptions; his figure for the Italian countryside was based on 5343 inscriptions.
52. Hopkins, ibid.
53. Angel, "Ecology," 94.
54. Bar-Ilan, "Infant Mortality."

to Tannaitic figures) and comparisons with premodern societies. He has conveniently organized all the references in his collection in a table that lists forty-six child deaths reported in the rabbinic literature, most of whom were males. But of the cases reported, nine of them happened to be children of Tannaim. Since there were—so Bar-Ilan—around 100 Tannaim in all and since half of them are mentioned in the sources "only sporadically," he divides the 100 Tannaim by two. He then surmises that the deaths of females were seldom reported and thus multiplies the number of deaths by two. These calculations leave him with 18/50 deaths per Tannaitic family or "more than 30 percent" (36 percent to be exact). Thus he concludes that this percentage on average died before age fourteen. Bar-Ilan then confirms his hypothesis by looking at comparisons with premodern societies where he finds similar child mortality rates.

Some might question these mathematical steps in logic but it is interesting that his figure is essentially in agreement with mine, which is based in skeletal remains. His percentage (36 percent) is somewhat lower than my 43 percent, but he only calculates for ages 0 to fourteen while I calculate for ages 0 to twenty. His figures and those of other demographers of the ancient world confirm that my estimates of child and youth mortality fall within the range of plausibility.

Life Expectancies

Another way of presenting the evidence is to assess life expectancies from birth and after reaching early adulthood. In addition to asking how many usually died before age five or age twenty, we can ask what would be the average life expectancy of a person born in ER Israel at birth and at adulthood. Some archaeologists and anthropologists have ventured such figures. I will first cite their calculations and then give mine based on my collection of the data.

Nagar and Torgeé, based on their excavation of the eight tombs in Judea in the Late Hellenistic and Early Roman periods, calculated that the average life expectancy from birth for all individuals was twenty-four years. Compare this figure with Greece (twenty-nine years)[55] and Egypt (twenty-four years)[56] during this same period—based on funerary inscriptions (Greece) and based on papyrus census records (Egypt)—and with the Coale-Demeny Life Table West for females,

55. Grmek, *Diseases*, 106.
56. Bagnall and Frier, *Demography*, 109.

which is, at birth, 22.5 years.[57] Frier states it was commonly accepted in scholarly circles at the time of his writing (1983) that a Roman life expectancy at birth was between twenty and thirty years.[58] So the results from the eight LH and ER tombs in Judea/Samaria are rather typical for the Greco-Roman world during this period. Further, Frier maintains, based on his collection of evidence throughout the Roman Empire, that on average 66 percent of children born died before age thirty.[59] In the eight Judean/Samaritan tombs, however, according to the raw data they supply, 54 percent died before age thirty.[60]

But we can compose our own life expectancy table from birth based on more data than just the eight tombs excavated by Nagar and Torgeé. We will gather information from ten different excavations consisting of hundreds of tombs and 987 individuals. The average life expectancy calculated in this way should be more accurate than simply using the data of Nagar and Torgeé since the sample size is larger. The table below shows the data.

Table G: Average Life Expectancy at Birth in the Late Hellenistic-Early Roman Periods in Palestine/Israel[61]

Site/tombs	Number of individuals	Total number of years lived
Caiaphas	51	540
Mount Scopus	70	949
Har Haẓofim Observatory	104	1000
Arnona	25	309
Naḥal Ḥever	17	327
Jericho	192	6335
French Hill (LH)	33	923
Giv'at ha-Mivtar	34	873

57. Ibid., 35.
58. Frier, "Pannonian Evidence"; so also Durand, "Mortality Estimates," 372.
59. Frier, "Pannonian Evidence," 328, based on Ulpian's life table.
60. Nagar and Torgeé, "Biological Characteristics," 167. But in their mortality curve below, they cal-culate 65.2 percent died before age thirty. Their mortality curve is not the same as simply working with the raw data since they opine that many infants' remains were unreadable and thus were underrepresented in the sample size. To compensate for this assumed factor, they used "life-table methodology" in constructing a mortality curve.
61. The table is composed based on the data given in: Arieli, "Har Haẓofim Observatory"; Zias, "Caiaphas"; Zias, "Mount Scopus"; Zias, "Arnona"; Nathan, "Naḥal Ḥever"; Arensburg and Smith, "Jewish Population"; Smith and Zias, "French Hill"; Haas, "Giv'at ha-Mivtar"; Nagar and Torgeé, "Biological Characteristics"; Smith, Bornemann, and Zias, "Skeletal Remains."

8 tombs in Judea/ Samaria excavated by Nagar and Torgeé	121	2363
Meiron	191	2363
En-Gedi	149	2579
Totals	**987**[62]	**19840**

These figures give us an average life expectancy from birth for both sexes of twenty years, somewhat lower than the calculations of Nagar and Torgeé, as well as that of the Coale-Demeny Life Table West for females.

Compare these life expectancies from birth with those today around the world: Japan (the highest) eighty-two years; United States seventy-eight years; Sierra Leone (the lowest) forty-six years.[63] Even the lowest life expectancy in today's world is more than twice that of the ancient Mediterranean person.

What about those reaching early adulthood? If one made it to age twenty, how long might one expect to live on average? There are two calculations given in the literature to which we may refer. Joe Zias[64] maintains that the average life span for the males examined at Qumran was thirty-four years. Nagar and Torgeé[65] calculated that the average life span for adults buried in the eight tombs of Judea/Samaria that they excavated was thirty-eight years. Compare these figures with that from Greece in the second century CE where the average was thirty-eight years for all persons examined, but with a significant gender gap: forty years for men, and thirty-four years for women.[66]

But, again, let us do our own calculation. We will add the total number of adult males and females in the Jerusalem tomb complexes

---

62. The figures for total individuals in the tombs may differ from table to table because, as is the case here, the anthropologists were sometimes uncertain of the age of an individual. Hence, these remains cannot be used to calculate average life expectancy from birth.

63. "List of Countries by Life Expectancy," *Wikipedia.* Online: https://en.wikipedia.org/wiki/List_of_countries_by_life_expectancy. Accessed Nov. 16, 2015. Compare *World Fact Book* operated by the United States C.I.A., which lists Monaco as having the longest life expectancy at eighty-nine years and Chad as having the shortest at forty-nine years: https://www.cia.gov/library/publications/the-world-factbook/rankorder/2102rank.html. Accessed Nov. 16, 2015.

64. Zias, "Cemeteries of Qumran."

65. Nagar and Torgeé, "Biological Characteristics."

66. Grmek, *Diseases,* 104. He actually gives several other calculations done in different ways. Compare these figures with Burn, "Hic breve vivitur," 16 who gives figures for several Roman provinces in the Byzantine period. The slave and freedman class of Carthage and the residents of the Danube provinces are close to our results: thirty-eight years (males), thirty-eight (females) and forty (males), thirty-three (females) respectively.

(Giv'at; Caiaphas; Scopus; French Hill; Akeldama; Arnona; and Abba), in Meiron in Galilee, in the Goliath family tomb at Jericho (tomb H), in Cave 8 at Naḥal Ḥever, the nine LH tombs at En-Gedi, and in the few excavated graves at Qumran where these are identified by age and sex. To arrive at a life expectancy figure, we will then divide this number into the total number of years of life.[67] The caution is that most of this evidence is from the Jerusalem area and has a much lower sample size[68] than the other two calculations: 146 males and 110 females.

Table H: Life Expectancy in Late Second Temple Israel from Adulthood (age 19)[69]

Location	Men	Women
Caiaphas tomb	142 years /4 persons	40 yrs /1 person
Mt. Scopus	411/12	437/15
Giv'at ha-Mivtar	381/9	348/10
French Hill LH	429/10	308/8
Akeldama	89/3	73/3
Arnona	30/1	157/4
Jericho-Goliath (tomb H)	474/11	280/7
Meiron	745/21	842/25
Qumran	802/19	52/6
Abba Cave	33/1	
Naḥal Ḥever	159/4	91/3
En-Gedi	1630/47	
Har Haẓofim	120/4	200/6
Totals	Average 5445/146 37 years	Average 3628/110 33 years

67. See Frier, "Roman Life Expectancy," 219 for the method of computing average life expectancy. Also cf. Grmek, *Diseases*, 105.
68. Why is the sample size so small in comparison with the two previous tables? Other reports of tomb excavations in Israel could not be used since they did not give this much data. We need an approximation of age at death and the identification of the sex of the individual. Where the anthropologists gave a range of ages (e.g., thirty-five to forty-five), I gave the average (hence, forty) for the purposes of the table.
69. The table is compiled from Arieli, "Har Haẓofim Observatory"; Steckoll, "Preliminary Excavation Report" (Qumran); Sheridan, "French Collection" (Qumran); Broshi and Eshel, "Whose Bones?" (Qumran); Smith, "Skeletal Remains (Abba cave)"; Smith and Zias, "French Hill (LH)"; Hachlili and Smith, "Goliath Family"; Smith, Bornemann, and Zias, "Skeletal Remains (Meiron)"; Zias, "Caiaphas"; Haas, "Giv'at ha-Mivtar"; Zias, "Arnona"; Zias, "Mount Scopus"; Arieli, "Har Haẓofim"; and Zias, "Anthropological Analysis (Akeldama)." One is unable to use much of the

We get the average of thirty-seven years life expectancy for any male reaching adulthood and thirty-three years life expectancy for females reaching adulthood in Israel in the late Second Temple period.

Compare these results with various calculations made by historians of Greece and Rome given in Table I:

Table I: Life expectancy at age 20—Various findings

HISTORIAN	AGE
Beloch[70]	Males: 36–37; Females: 30–31
Russell[71]	Males: 49.4; Females: 47.7
Angel[72]	Males: 42; Females 31
Angel[73] (25 years later)	Males: 40.2; Females 34.3
Coale-Demeny Life Table West[74]	Females: 49.9
Gallant[75]	Males: 40; Females 38
Zias (Qumran)	Males: 34 years
Nagar and Torgeé (8 Judean/Samaritan tombs)	All: 38 years
Grmek[76]	Males: 40; Females 34

The calculations above in Table H, then, are a bit lower than those based on evidence elsewhere in the Mediterranean world (Table I) and obtained not only from osteoarchaeological methods but also from epigraphical.

One feature confronts us immediately from our calculation: There was a significant gender gap in life expectancy for those reaching early adulthood (also reported by most of the historians in Table I). Wells affirmed that on average one could demonstrate a gap using both osteological and epigraphic evidence of five years life expectancy.[77]

Why the disparity in sexes? Most point to the dangers of childbirth

---

osteoarchaeological data in this calculation due to: some publications did not calculate the ages beyond the most general observation: "child, adult, etc." (Arensburg and Rak, "French Hill" [ER] and Arensburg and Smith, "Jericho") and some did not give the sex of the individual (Nagar and Torgeé, "Biological Characteristics").

70. See Russell, *Late Ancient*, 25.
71. Ibid., 64.
72. Angel, "Length of Life," 20.
73. Angel, "Ecology," 94.
74. Bagnall and Frier, *Demography*, 35.
75. Gallant, *Risk*, 20.
76. Grmek, *Diseases*, 104.
77. Wells, "Ancient Obstetric," 1235.

in this nonmedical age.[78] Burn suggests that it was more about exhaustion. Giving birth, nursing infants, and doing all the daily required labor simply wore out the mothers.[79] Wells tried to establish that it was preferential feeding of boys over girls. The girls were undernourished and thus in young adulthood unable to survive.[80] Whatever the cause,[81] in antiquity most men outlived women. Today, of course, that is reversed.

We noted at the beginning of our presentation that there were three agreed-upon results of the study of ancient demographics:

1. Infant mortality was shockingly high by today's standards.
2. Even if one should reach the age of twenty, the life expectancy was still pretty low (somewhere in the mid-thirties to early forties; see Table I).
3. There was a significant gap in the life expectancy of women and men (see Table I).

Our own findings from the 1475 individuals represented in the LH and ER tombs of Israel confirm those results.

Implications for New Testament Research

What do all of these data mean in human terms? What must it be like to live in such conditions? Walter Scheidel[82] gives a helpful overview of Greco-Roman population in antiquity:

---

78. Russell, *Late Ancient*, 35; Gallant, *Risk*, 20; Eakins, "Human Osteology," 95; and Demand, *Birth*, 76–86. Demand maintains that childbirth, before the modern age, was absolutely perilous. The main causes of death in mothers before giving birth, during delivery, and also in the days after giving birth were puerperal fever, toxemia, hemorrhage, and malaria. Stark, *Rise of Christianity*, 120 emphasizes specifically inept abortions.
79. Burn, "Hic breve vivitur," 12. Burn writes that ancient mothers "combine in one organism the functions of the milk-cow and the draught ox." His table on p. 16 lists average life expectancies of males and females from several different provinces in Africa and Europe. Some are as much as ten years longer (N.W. Africa) but some are just about identical to our figures: Carthage and the Danube provinces. Grmek agrees with Burn (*Diseases*, 89).
80. Wells, "Ancient Obstetric."
81. On the other hand, Durand ("Mortality estimates," 369) opines that women did not usually die as young as their tombstones indicate since they, similar to our modern vanities, would have wanted to "appear young." So, their families would represent them as dying younger than they actually did and falsify the age at death on the tombstone. Angel, "Length of Life," 20–21 suggested that certain soil conditions might have skewed the evidence (viz. of the skeletal remains).
82. Scheidel, "Population and Demography."

1. Infant mortality was around 30 percent (for the first year of life).
2. Half of all people died before they were old enough to bear or father children.
3. Death was as much a phenomenon of childhood as of old age.
4. Ancient populations were necessarily very young.

Such factors resulted, according to Scheidel, in the following socio-economic conditions:

1. Destabilization of families.
2. Ubiquity of widows[83] and orphans.
3. Disincentives to investment in education.
4. Disruption of trust networks that sustain commerce.

These are very helpful conclusions for us to start with. I hope here to expand on them a bit. I see the following five implications of the above data for our understanding of the New Testament:

1. There was mourning in every household over dead children.
2. There were many single-parent families.
3. There was a shortage of young workers.
4. There must have been pressure to marry and procreate early in life.
5. There was a lack of mentorship for the young.

A Household of Grief

Such high child mortality must have meant that death, mourning, and sadness were a reality for every family almost constantly. This reality is presented to us frequently in the Gospels where families are often mourning a dead child or showing anxiety over the illness of a child.[84] We have a saying in the western culture that, "No parent should have to bury a child." That saying would be meaningless in this society. What is a rather rare tragedy in our society—losing a child—was the experience of the overwhelming majority of families. And they did not lose just one child but several. One can see traces of these conditions

83. Or, I would add, widowers.
84. Russell, *Late Ancient*, 35: "If a family had six children, it would have to expect that the first would die as a baby, the second by twenty, the third by thirty-five to forty, the fourth by forty-five to fifty, the fifth, by sixty and the sixth later." If anything, Russell's calculations are too optimistic. According to our calculations not two but probably three children would die before age twenty. Of the three left, one or two would die before age forty.

in the New Testament Gospels: There are references to sick children (Mark 9:17–18; Luke 8:42, 49; 9:42; John 4:49[85]) and to instances where young persons have died (Mark 5:35; Luke 7:12; John 11:14). We may have read these accounts in the past and regarded them as in our own life experiences, as tragic but rare. From the skeletal evidence, however, we know these occurrences must have been, though still tragic, not at all rare. They were not the exception but the rule. Thus, when we see mothers bringing their children (infants in Luke 18:15–17) for Jesus to bless, we may presume, as Richard Rohrbaugh suggests, that they are "being brought by frightened mothers seeking healing or protection for their babies, many of whom will likely die."[86]

Based on my calculations above—and confirmed by those of others from elsewhere in the empire—if a couple gave birth to ten children (not at all an unusual occurrence), three of them would die before reaching age five and a fourth before age twenty. Of the remaining six children, three more would die before their mid-thirties. Only three of the ten could expect to live past age forty. Further, shortly after the birth of the tenth child, one would expect one of the parents to die leaving the surviving parent with six children to rear alone.

Single-Parent Families

Second, a life expectancy, even for those reaching young adulthood, of mid-thirties to early forties would mean that there would be small children still at home when one (or both) parents had died. Many families must have been missing parents from the nucleated family. If an Egyptian comparison may be offered here, it is telling: Bagnall and Frier[87] calculate—based on their mortality studies of the census records—that there was a one-in-four chance that one or even both of the parents would die within ten years of marriage. Where the census records show age at death of the spouse, they indicate that the survivors were rather young (in their twenties and early thirties). Further, in the eight cases they looked at where the death of the spouse was expressly stated in the census report, only three of the men remarried while none of the women had remarried.[88]

85. Compare the story in John with b. Ber. 34b.
86. Rohrbaugh, "Introduction," 5.
87. Bagnall and Frier, Demography, 123.
88. Ibid. Incidentally, the same sort of remarriage rates held for divorces (p. 124): of the nine cases they sampled, only two of the nine males had remarried and none of the eight females. They also seemed to divorce young: Men: age 22, 31, 32, and 37—and some whose ages were not given. Women: age 29 (2×) 33, 40, 49, and 57—and some whose ages were not given.

Such conditions meant, surely, that there were many single-parent families and that nucleated families were often forced to rely on the extended family for security. The nucleated family needed the extended family to rear the children and to provide a safety net. But in this period the *bet 'av* (see pp. 82–85, ch 3) probably no longer existed as it had in the Israelite period.[89] The safety net was no longer there. This would have meant that many children were reared by an aunt or uncle—or by an older sibling—since grandparents likely were not around either.[90] Doubtless, many children roamed the streets, unattended, like urchins or waifs. Perhaps this possibility changes our imagining the scene depicted in Mark 10:13–16 (Matt 19:14/Luke 18:16/ GT 22) in which people are bringing children to Jesus to receive a blessing and he announces that these "waifs are typical of the Kingdom of God."

Shortage of Young Workers

Further, there probably were not enough young men and women to do the farm work or craft work. That means children themselves must have done some of the work. One can imagine that people began laboring early in life and just never stopped. What we regard as a childhood—a time of play and imagination—did not happen for the majority of ancient children. They had to work, especially if one of the parents had died.[91] Hiring out one's child for wages (and even selling one's child into slavery) has a long history in the Ancient Near East.[92] Needy families were often forced to utilize whatever resources were at their disposal and, unfortunately, the children were sometimes the only resource.

Pressure to Procreate Early in Life

Such short life spans also meant that people needed to marry young and procreate abundantly. In a world with such high child mortality, it takes at least six children per family to maintain the population. Two to three of the six children would die before reaching adulthood and one of the surviving three would die in his/her twenties.

---

89. See Fiensy, *Social History*, 126–32.
90. See Reed, "Instability."
91. As Scheidel ("Real Wages") argues, even when there were both parents, the children often had to work to bring full subsistence to the family, especially if the parents were day laborers.
92. See Garroway, *Children*, 113–40 (debt slavery for children), 155–58 (hireling children).

The stress on the parents must have been intense. Living with the knowledge that your children could die in any given year—indeed that some of them almost certainly would die—would be very scary.[93] The scripture quoted in Matthew and applied to the infants of Bethlehem (Matt 2:18, quoting Jer 31:15) might easily be a standing description of ancient villages throughout the Roman Empire. There would be mourning and weeping; a mother would be weeping for her children almost every day somewhere in the village.

So frequent was infant mortality that one passage in the Talmud (b. Mo'ed Qat. 24a) makes the following distinctions in burial customs: Infants under thirty days old are carried to the cemetery in their mothers' arms. They do not "form a line of mourners" for this child and they do not recite the prayer for the mourners. Infants between the ages of thirty days and twelve months are carried to the cemetery in a small box. They do form the line of mourners and recite the benediction for the mourners. Infants over twelve months old are carried to the cemetery on a bier and the community can show public signs of grief. A poor child (since children are the sole pleasure of poor people) may be lamented after the age of three (or some rabbis said after age five). A wealthy child may be lamented only after age five (or some rabbis said after age six). Such rules, it seems, were designed to control the grief and lamentation which otherwise might be overwhelming.[94]

Anecdotal Evidence

Anecdotal evidence might help put a face on this data. Cornelia (the mother of the Gracchi) bore twelve children. All survived their father but only three survived childhood (the two famous brothers and one sister).[95] Quintilian lamented the loss of his young wife and two young sons (who died at ages four and nine). Fronto and his wife had six children but only one daughter survived. Marcus Aurelius and his wife Faustina had at least twelve children, of whom only one son, Commodus, lived to adulthood.[96] With child mortality that high, mourning entered every household almost every year.

The rabbinic literature also indicates a high child mortality. There are many references to children dying in the Talmudic and Midrashic

93. See Raaj K. Sah, "Child Mortality Changes." The "parental welfare" becomes better when child mortality decreases according to Sah.
94. See Garroway, *Children*, 243.
95. Plutarch, *Tib. Gracch.* 16.3.
96. Suetonius, *Gaius* 7; Quintillian, *Inst. Or.* 6; Parkin, *Demography*, 94.

literature. Especially tragic was the fact that often more than one child in the family died at nearly the same time,[97] evidently due to communicable diseases. Further, there are even references to as many as ten of a family's children having died[98] before reaching adulthood. Losing that many children did not inoculate the parents from grief. The mourning would be very intense as one Talmudic story demonstrates.[99]

The Few Elderly

All of this is not, of course, to say that everyone died in his/her thirties or forties. There are many alleged octogenarians and nonagenarians: Parkin and Grmek list several philosophers, political leaders, historians, poets, and rhetoricians who died in their nineties. They can even find a few (e.g., Democritus, age 104; Gorgias of Leontini, age 107) who eclipsed the century mark. Grmek notes that the oldest attested age on a Greek funerary inscription is 110 years.[100] In Christian tradition, we read of several elderly persons: A lady named Anna was eighty-four years old (Luke 2:37). Polycarp, the bishop of Smyrna, was said to have lived into his eighties before he died by martyrdom.[101] The apostle John allegedly lived into the reign of Trajan,[102] which would have made him probably past ninety years old. But a few exceptions do not change the overall conditions. Very few lived to such an age.

The (rare) appearance of the elderly as reported in the literature is supported by the Mortality Curve of Nagar and Torgeé, based on the excavation of the Judean and Samaritan tombs dating from the Hellenistic to the Early Roman periods. They constructed their graph based on the data from the tombs of two of their sites in Judea (comprising six tombs) to show the percentage of the population that died by age groups. The Mortality Curve below and Table J are calculated based on a "life-table methodology." They assumed that several infant remains (under one year old) were undeterminable and thus underrepresented. Hence to make the analysis more accurate they used the life-table methodology, following Coal-Demeny Life Table West.[103]

---

97. See b. Moed Qatan 28b; b. Moed Qatan 21b; Midrash Mishlei 31:10; b. Taan. 13b; and Bar-Ilan, "Infant Mortality."
98. As happened to R. Yehonan (b. ber 5a–b). See Bar-Ilan, "Infant Mortality."
99. See b. Sanh. 104b where one woman grieved so over the death of a child that R. Gamliel, her neighbor, wept in sympathy until "his eyelashes fell out." See Bar-Ilan, "Infant Mortality."
100. Parkin Demography, 107; Grmek, Diseases, 109.
101. Martyrdom IX.
102. Irenaeus, Against Heresies, 3.3.
103. Nagar and Torgeé, "Biological Characteristics," 167.

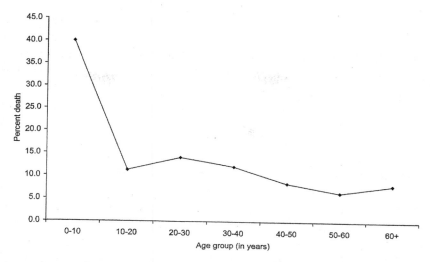

Fig. 4.2 The Mortality Curve of Two Hellenistic-Early Roman Jewish Populations in Israel. Reproduced by permission of the *Israel Exploration Journal* and the authors. The two populations were the villages of Tel Ḥadid and Shoham. They omitted the other two villages since their remains were difficult to assign ages to.

Their precise percentages for this population are as follows:

Table J[104]

Age interval (years)	Percentage of deaths
0–9	40
10–19	11.2
20–29	14
30–39	12
40–49	8.4
50–59	6.4
60	8

Notice the high mortality in the 0 to nine years age-cohort. In this mortality curve, 40 percent of the children died before age ten, 11.2 percent more died by age twenty, and a total of 65.2 percent died before age thirty. This youth mortality rate (51.2 percent), then, is a bit higher

104. Adapted from Nagar and Torgeé, ibid., 166–67, Table 3.

than the average for Israel at this time according to our earlier calculations (44 percent).

The Mortality Curve gives us an overview of how many in the two sites died every ten years and how many survived into their sixties and beyond. It offers a suggestion as to the life cycle and population profile of a typical Palestinian/Israeli village in this period. But since it is based on so little evidence (153 individuals), we can only say at this point that it is suggestive. Still, it shows that some persons (8 percent) lived into old age. The point here is that there were not many over sixty years of age buried in the tombs, but there were a few.

The lack of mentorship from older men and women is a constant in societies with high child mortality rates. Patricia Smith observes that there is a correlation between high infant mortality and death in early adult life. Where infant mortality is high, very few adults survive past fifty years.[105] Smith offers several age group comparisons based on multiple tomb excavations in Israel. The two relevant for our purpose: En-Gedi and Jericho (because of their date) show a ratio of around two to one in terms of young adults (ages twenty to forty-nine) to older adults (over fifty). There would have been few older mentors or role models for young adults. As Jonathan Reed observes,[106] virtually no young man knew his grandfather and very few still had a living father. This situation created a restless class of (to us) younger men roaming about Galilee without "adult" supervision, exactly what we see in the Gospels.

This all makes one wonder about Jesus's family. Was Jesus in a single-parent family? Was he reared by his mother? His father certainly disappears from the Gospels when Jesus is an adult. Did he start to labor early in life? Perhaps his "carpentry" began as a boy (Mark 6:3) and by the time we meet him, he has already been doing a full day's work for twenty-five years or more.

In light of such short life spans, Jesus's assigned age (by Luke 3:23[107]) of "about" thirty years does not really seem so young. It would be more in harmony with this data to envision Jesus and his disciples as, though

---

105. Smith, "Approach," 5. The converse is also true. Where infant mortality is low, it is probable that the population will survive past age fifty ("Approach," 7).
106. Reed, "Instability."
107. Though if one calculates a probable birth for Jesus of between 6 and 4 BCE and takes the chronological note in Luke 3:1 seriously (that Jesus began his ministry in the fifteenth year of Tiberius's reign), it makes Jesus more like thirty-two to thirty-four years old. Shimon Gibson, *Cave of John the Baptist*, 132, suggests that Jesus was thirty-four years old at the beginning of his ministry. Marshall, *Luke*, 162, thinks the reference in b Sanh. 106b to Balaam's age at death as thirty-three or thirty-four years is a coded reference to Jesus's age.

rather young by our standards, middle-aged. We often ask what happened to the rest of the Twelve Disciples not mentioned in the New Testament. Only Peter and John are featured (Gal 2:9; 1 Cor 9:5; James is said to have been martyred early; Acts 12:2) while the others disappear from the New Testament (though are featured in noncanonical literature).[108] The short answer is that most of them probably died early. When the average life expectancy of an adult male was thirty-seven years, we cannot imagine that all of the Twelve, except those martyred, lived to old age.

Finally, what was it like for this company, where life was so brief and often so full of grief, to hear the words in the Gospels? The Beatitudes take on an enhanced meaning: "Blessed are those who mourn ... Blessed are those who hunger and thirst for justice ..." (Matt 5:4, 6). How did the numerous promises of "rest" and "life" sound to them (e.g., Matt 8:28; John 10:10)? How did all those references to the "kingdom of God" and to the "age to come" resonate? It reminds one of the twelfth-century CE Christian hymn by Bernard of Morlaix:

Hic breve vivitur,	Brief life is here our portion,
hic breve plangitur,	Brief sorrow, short-lived care;
hic breve fletur.	The life that knows no ending,
Non breve vivere,	The tearless life, is there.[110]
non breve plangere,	
retribuetur.[109]	

Brief lifetimes were the norm before the modern era in virtually every society. Such high child mortality and such brief adult life spans must have made the folk in the New Testament era—as also this hymn writer—that much keener to think about what lay beyond.

---

108. E.g., Thomas appears in many texts, especially of Syrian origin.
109. Text in Moorsom, *Historical Companion*, 124. Literally: "Here it is briefly lived; here briefly grieved; here briefly wept. Not to live briefly, not to grieve briefly, will be restored."
110. Bernard, *De Contemptu Mundi.* Translation by J. M. Neale.

5

Conclusions: What Archaeology Can and Cannot Do

It is very interesting and just plain good fun to rummage through another person's things. Archaeology is, in a way, like climbing into someone's attic and exploring their old trunk. One can look at faded, black-and-white photographs, outdated clothing styles, yellowed newspaper clippings, and relics such as dried-up baseball gloves, tarnished trophies, and moth-eaten military uniforms. But in examining all of these items, a person can piece together a life (or lives). Certainly the puzzle pieces are not all there. The "researcher" must use a lot of imagination and must have knowledge that goes beyond what is in the attic. It helps—for example, if the lives were lived in the 1920s, 30s, and 40s—to know what was going on in this country and in the wider world at that time. Then that old military uniform makes good sense. One member of the family fought in the Second World War, and you can imagine how the family felt when their child went off to war. It is even possible that the son or daughter did not survive the conflict. With the artifact (the uniform), perhaps some newspaper clippings, and knowledge of the wider historical context, a person can, with a little imagination, begin to relive the family's experience.

The study of archaeology is a lot like our attic researcher. It takes other persons' surviving items, considers these items in the context of the wider world, and pieces together lives. Sometimes, archaeology also itself expands and clarifies the "wider world." The problem is that what archaeologists find is seldom as complete and detailed as what might be in a family's attic. If archaeology can give us fascinating results, it is also limited in what it can do.

What Archaeology Cannot Do

1. Archaeology cannot prove or disprove the Bible.[1] Having archaeology prove or disprove the Bible is like police officers interviewing witnesses of a car accident. They will ask what happened, when it happened, and who did it. Then they will check the weather conditions, the time of day, and skid marks to see if the witnesses' stories are plausible or implausible. Did the red car skid and hit the blue car or was it the other way round? Was it dark or rainy? One can only show the plausibility (unless, of course, there are several video recordings of the accident) of the witnesses' recollection.

Archaeology also can only do that. Rather than actually proving or disproving the Bible, it can only help us determine if the story is plausible or implausible. We saw in chapter 2 that when it "proves" the Bible it usually only confirms part of the story (e.g., Shishak) and makes it probable that some event *like* that narrated in the biblical text actually happened or that a person something *like* the one described in the text actually lived. When it "disproves" the Bible (e.g., the exodus story) it only shows that the story as it is understood now—assuming the consensus dating—is implausible. But perhaps, as we stated in chapter 2, if one assumes a different date, the story becomes more credible. If archaeology's "proof" of the Bible is often ambiguous, so sometimes is its "disproof." As one of the great archaeologists of the twentieth century, Roland de Vaux, wrote: "[T]he 'confirmation' brought by archaeology to the biblical narrative is rarely without ambiguity."[2]

Some of the best thinking on the uses and abuses of archaeology came at the seam of the paradigm shifts in the twentieth century

---

1. The two undertakings are really the same thing, as Hawkins offers: "Since archaeologists did not find evidence of the biblical events of Jericho at Tell es-Sultan, then the biblical account has been disproved. D. Merling observes that 'the logic and corollary to this logic would be: the truthfulness of the biblical text has been disproved by archaeology; therefore, it is also possible that archaeology could have proved the truthfulness of the Bible'" (*Israel*, 101). If one can "prove" the Bible by using archaeology, then one can also disprove it. Likewise, if one can "disprove" the Bible by archaeology, one can also prove it.
2. De Vaux, "Right and Wrong," 77.

when the discipline of archaeology passed from the dominance of W. F. Albright and his school into the "New Archaeology" (see chapter 1). Then archaeologists whose views were being criticized had to rethink their positions. In a seminal essay, George Ernest Wright wrote about what archaeology can and cannot do. Wright observed:

> With regard to Biblical events, however, it cannot be overstressed that archaeological data are mute. Fragmentary ruins, preserving only a tiny fraction of the full picture of ancient life, cannot speak without someone asking questions of them. . . . Archaeology can *prove* very little about anything without minds stored with a wide-ranging variety of information which carefully begin to ask questions of the mute remains in order to discover what they mean. [Archaeological data] must be analyzed in a variety of ways, and then with all other data available, its meaning in the overall picture of a cultural continuum is expressed by interpretation.[3]

In other words, the ruins themselves do not prove or disprove anything. They cannot speak; we, the interpreters, must speak for them. The question is "What do the ruins mean?" The answer to that question is determined by the interpretation given the ruins by the historians; and historians will often disagree. Again, Roland de Vaux wrote, "Archaeology does not confirm the text . . . it can only confirm the interpretation which we give it."[4] We might state it like this: When we maintain that archaeology confirms or contradicts the Bible, what we really mean is that our interpretation of the material remains confirms or contradicts our interpretation of the text.

Furthermore, the interpretations are determined by the questions that the archaeologists and historians ask. The questions determine the interpretation as G. E. Wright maintained. But the problem is that one generation's questions may not be the same questions as the next generation's questions:

> [T]he kind of questions asked are part and parcel of the answers "heard" because of predispositions on the part of the questioner. . . . [but] One generation's questions may not be another's, and in every case the questions asked are integral to the answers.[5]

2. Archaeology alone cannot tell us all we want to know about the biblical world. We need texts. Without texts, archaeology is like a person watch-

---

3. Wright, "Archaeology," 73, 76.
4. De Vaux, "Right and Wrong," 78.
5. Wright, "Archaeology," 73–74.

ing a film with the sound turned off. One can see the movie, and make out in general the course of the events (someone is in danger, etc.) but cannot make out why all of these things are happening. On the other hand, just having texts with no artifacts is like watching the same film with the sound on but with your eyes shut. The viewer can hear the words and gain meaning as to the why of things, but many things expressed in facial movement and action scenes will not be understood. As one of those texts (or rather as a huge collection of texts), the Bible is indispensable in helping us understand its own milieu. Alongside the Bible, we must read the cuneiform tablets from Mesopotamia, Syria, and Asia Minor, the hieroglyphics from Egypt, the Apocrypha, the Pseudepigrapha, the Rabbinic literature, Josephus, the Dead Sea Scrolls, the Nag Hammadi texts, the Greco-Roman literature, and the inscriptions from many parts of the Mediterranean and Middle Eastern regions. Without the literature we might develop a misunderstanding as to what a site, building ruin, or other item means. The artifacts and the texts must cooperate in our interpretation of events and subsequently in our writing of history.

3. *It cannot tell us if the Bible is right or true (theologically).* Archaeology is simply the study of the things that survived the ravages of time. Such a study cannot decide religious and theological truth. As Dever wrote more than twenty-five years ago:

> [A]rchaeology, insofar as it is a historical discipline, is uniquely equipped to help answer such questions in Biblical studies as these: What likely took place? When did it occur? Who were the principal participants? How did it happen? But here archaeology reaches the limits of its inquiry. It cannot, and is not intended to, answer the question, Why?—certainly not in terms of ultimate or divine causes.[6]

So, archaeology can, at best, demonstrate the plausibility of biblical events and characters. But even if archaeology could confirm almost all—or even all—of the events referred to in the Bible, it would not, therefore, "prove" the Bible. The Bible is a collection of religious books making theological claims. As de Vaux argued, "The truth of the Bible is of a religious order . . . [it cannot] be confirmed or invalidated by the material discoveries of archaeology."[7] No artifact—i.e., no stone,

---

6. Dever, *Recent Archaeological*, 35.
7. De Vaux, "Right and Wrong," 68. Cf. McRay, *Archaeology*, 19–20: "[Archaeology] cannot prove the New Testament to be either theologically inspired or historically accurate. . . . Proving that Mecca and Medina existed in the sixth and seventh centuries in western Arabia does not prove that Mohammed lived there or that the Koran is true."

no potsherd, no coin, no tool, no building ruin—can demonstrate that such claims are "true or false," whatever definition one uses for truth. The "New Archaeology" was correct, even if the members of that movement did go a bit too far.

What Archaeology Can Do

1. *Archaeology can help us reconstruct the social, economic, household, and material environment.* Archaeology cooperates with texts (and sometimes cultural anthropology) to help us imagine the story. Thus one asks, what would the teachings of Jesus—especially as we have them presented to us in the source commonly called Q—have meant to a family that had lost several children to disease? What might those words mean to a young wife and mother whose husband had just died, leaving her with four or five children? How should we understand some of those teachings in light of the information on child mortality and longevity that chapter 4 presented? Here archaeology considered alongside the literature is of great importance.

But one must enter into this investigation with caution. Sometimes archaeologists can give conclusions too soon. It takes many years of patient digging to get a good idea of what is "down below." What looks like a sure conclusion is often reversed years later. For example, many spoke too soon about the nature of first-century CE Galilee and envisaged quite a different place than most do now. They thought Galilee was very Hellenized and that there were surely Cynic philosophers pounding the pavement in the cities of Sepphoris and Tiberias. These "conclusions" then had a significant impact on the historical Jesus research.[8] Another example is Yizhar Hirschfeld's excavations of the ruins at Ramat ha-Nadiv (see chapter 2). Initially—for years—he thought the site was something quite different (a fortress) than what he finally recognized it to have been: a mansion and large estate.[9] Remains come to light slowly and haphazardly, and the first results may be deceiving.

2. *It can occasionally (rarely in my opinion) directly change our interpretation of a specific text or verse in the Bible.* As I wrote in chapter 2, mostly,

8. See Mack, *Myth*, 66. Mack wrote that Galilee was "thoroughly Hellenized." Of course, nearly every place in the Mediterranean world was Hellenized in some sense (technology and architecture, not to mention the spread of the Greek language). But does using Greek architecture in your town also mean your citizens accept Greek philosophy? See Fiensy, *Jesus*, 61–62.
9. See Hirschfeld, "Bath and Fortress"; and Hirschfeld and Feinberg-Vamosh, "Country Gentleman's Estate."

archaeology provides context or background from which the interpreter can picture the narrative. Indeed, to expect archaeology to be able to interpret individual verses or texts assumes a certain view of scripture: scripture as a collection of propositional statements. Rather, in my view, scripture is more about a metanarrative that is told by many smaller narratives (some of which disagree with each other). Archaeology as context mostly helps us to imagine the story(ies).

Yet, there are some interpretations in the Bible that change directly as a result of an artifact. Usually these artifacts are texts. For example, the Ugaritic texts have led some scholars to offer dramatically different translations (and understandings) of certain Old Testament books. One example of this phenomenon is Mitchel Dahood's commentary on the Psalms. His many novel translations of phrases, based on the cuneiform tablets from the ancient Syrian city of Ugarit, have offered fresh insights to interpreters.[10] Many of the phrases from the Dead Sea Scrolls have also greatly benefited New Testament interpreters.[11] But such verse-by-verse insight coming from *nonwritten* artifacts ranges from the rare to the nonexistent.

3. It can offer confirmation (or contradiction) of a text, event, or person of the Bible. Confirmation of the historicity of these items is not proving them. Although the confirmation (or contradiction) is usually rather ambiguous, there are still some interesting "convergences" (to use Dever's term). Inquiring minds naturally want to know about such things. I, for one, do not think it is either scientifically or theologically improper to ask about these issues. I think of the history of the quest for the historical Jesus as an example. The quest went through a period in which scholars argued that it was invalid to ask about the historical Jesus. Either it was an attempt, they argued, to prove who Jesus was or it was an attempt to disprove Christianity.[12] But this view could not dominate for long; historians and persons in general refused to be dictated to about this issue. It is a natural curiosity to ask what Jesus actually did and said. The same is true for other biblical events and persons. Did King David actually exist? I do not see that as an improper ques-

---

10. Dahood, *Psalms*, I.17, characterizes his commentary more as "a translation and philological commentary which utilizes the linguistic information offered by the Ras Shamra (i.e. Ugaritic) tablets." See also the translation of the Hebrew word פים referred to in chapter 1.

11. See e.g. David Flusser, *Judaism*. One might also consider Klassen, "Judas and Jesus," who thinks that an inscription on a glass drinking vessel changes our interpretation of Matt 26:50.

12. See for a summary of the history of the quest: Theissen and Merz, *Historical Jesus*, 5–6; and Wright, *Victory*, 22.

tion. Sometimes archaeology can provide some data for us to use in our interpreted answer to such questions.

So, we descend from our make-believe attic with our artifacts: the faded photos, the yellowed newspaper clippings, the moth-eaten army uniform, and the dried-up baseball glove. None would consider these items valuable. But taken together, in the context of what we know about the wider world of the 1920–40s they tell a moving story of a typical kid from a small town who went off to fight in the most brutal war in history and who perhaps gave his/her life. For years the old photos and baseball glove were all his parents had to remember their little girl or boy. Seen in this way, these artifacts are priceless because they help us relive someone's human story. This is how archaeology helps us interpret the Bible.

Appendix: Archaeological Periods of Palestine (Neolithic to Iron Age)

Pre-Pottery Neolithic A[1]	8500–7500 BCE
Pre-Pottery Neolithic B	7500–6000 BCE
Pottery Neolithic A	6000–5000 BCE
Pottery Neolithic B	5000–4300 BCE
Chalcolithic	4300–3300 BCE
Early Bronze I	3300–3050 BCE
Early Bronze II–III	3050–2300 BCE
Early Bronze IV/Middle Bronze I	2300–2000 BCE
Middle Bronze IIA	2000–1800/1750 BCE
Middle Bronze IIB–C	1800/1750–1550 BCE
Late Bronze I	1550–1400 BCE
Late Bronze IIA–B	1400–1200 BCE
Iron IA	1200–1150 BCE
Iron IB	1150–1000 BCE
Iron IIA	1000–925 BCE
Iron IIB	925–720 BCE
Iron IIC	720–586 BCE
Persian	586–333 BCE

1. From A. Mazar, *Archaeology of the Land of the Bible*, 30; and Fiensy and Strange, *Galilee I*, ix.

Hellenistic I	333–152 BCE
Hellenistic II	152–37 BCE
Early Roman	37 BCE–70 CE
Middle Roman	70–250 CE
Late Roman	250–363 CE

Bibliography

Abegg Jr., Martin, Peter Flint, and Eugene Ulrich. *The Dead Sea Scrolls Bible.* New York: HarperCollins, 1999.

Adams, Samuel L. *Social and Economic Life in Second Temple Judea.* Louisville: Westminster John Knox, 2014.

Adan-Bayewitz, David. *Common Pottery in Roman Galilee.* Ramat-Gan, Israel: Bar-Ilan University Press, 1993.

_____. "Kefar Hananya, 1986." *IEJ* 37 (1987): 178–79.

Adan-Bayewitz, David, and I. Perlman. "The Local Trade of Sepphoris in the Roman Period." *IEJ* 40 (1990): 153–72.

Aḥituv, Shmuel, Esther Eshel, and Ze'ev Meshel. "The Inscriptions." Pages 73–142 in Ze'ev Meshel, editor. *Kuntillet 'Ajrud (Ḥorvat Teman): An Iron Age II Religious Site on the Judah-Sinai Border.* Jerusalem: Israel Exploration Society, 2012.

Albright, William Foxwell. *The Archaeology of Palestine.* Gloucester, MA: Peter Smith, 1971.

_____. *From Stone Age to Christianity.* Baltimore: Johns Hopkins University Press, 1957.

Amerding, Carl Edwin. "Shalmaneser, Black Obelisk of." Page 409 in Edward M. Blaiklock and R. K. Harrison, editors. *IDB (New).* Grand Rapids: Zondervan, 1983.

Amiry, Suad, and Vera Tamari. *The Palestinian Village Home.* London: British Museum, 1989.

Angel, J. Lawrence. "Ecology and Population in the Eastern Mediterranean." *World Archaeology* 4, no. 1 (1972): 88–105.

_____. "Length of Life in Ancient Greece." *Journal of Gerontology* 2 (1947): 18–24.

Arensburg, B., and Anna Belfer-Cohen. "Preliminary Report on the Skeletal Remains from the 'En Gedi Tombs." *Atiqot* 24 (1994): 12–14.

Arensburg, B., and Patricia Smith. "Anthropological Tables." Pages 192–94 in Rachel Hachlili and Ann E. Killebrew, editors. *Jericho: The Jewish Cemetery of the Second Temple Period.* Jerusalem: Israel Antiquities Authority, 1999.

Arensburg, B., and Y. Rak. "Skeletal Remains of an Ancient Jewish Population from French Hill, Jerusalem." *BASOR* 219 (1975): 69–71.

_____. "Appendix: the Jewish Population of Jericho 100 BC-70AD." *PEQ* 115 (1983): 133–39.

Arieli, Rotem. "Human Remains from the Har Haẓofim Observatory Tombs (Mt. Scopus, Jerusalem)." *Atiqot* 35 (1998): 37–42.

Arnold, Clinton E. "'I Am Astonished That You Are So Quickly Turning Away!' (Gal 1:6): Paul and Anatolian Folk Belief." *NTS* 51 (2005): 429–49.

Aviam, Mordechai. "'Kefar Hananya Ware' Made in Yodefat: Pottery Production at Yodefat in the First Century AD." Pages 139–46 in Bettina Fischer-Genz, Yvonne Gerber, and Hanna Hamel, editors. *Roman Pottery in the Near East: Local Production and Regional Trade.* Oxford: Archaeopress, 2014.

_____. "Yodefat-Jotapata." Pages 109–26 in David A. Fiensy and James Riley Strange, editors. *Galilee in the Late Second Temple and Mishnaic Periods II: The Archaeological Record from Cities, Towns, and Villages.* Minneapolis: Fortress Press, 2015.

Badè, William Frederick. *A Manual of Excavation in the Near East: Methods of Digging and Recording at the Tell en-Nasbeh Expedition in Palestine.* Berkeley: University of California Press, 1934. Online: https://books.google.com/books?id=wXvMsN4IejoC&pg=PA4&lpg=PA4&dq=gezer+excavation+manual&source=bl&ots=rwZVJmSH6r&sig=Tmc8QP3MZFim2pK8QYvg23gT8vA&hl=en&sa=X&ved=0ahUKEwixpoXgrNnMAhWC5yYKHXL0D-EQ6AEIJTAE#v=onepage&q=gezer%20excavation%20manual&f=false. Accessed May 14, 2016.

Bagnall, Roger S., and Bruce W. Frier. *The Demography of Roman Egypt.* Cambridge: Cambridge University Press, 1994.

Bar-Adon, Pessaḥ. "Another Settlement of the Judean Desert Sect at 'En el-Ghuweir on the Shores of the Dead Sea." *BASOR* 227 (1977): 1–25.

Bar-Ilan, Meir. "Infant Mortality in the Land of Israel in Late Antiquity." Pages 3–25 in S. Fishbane and J. Lightstone, editors. *Judaism and Jewish Society.* Montreal: Concordia University Press, 1990. Online: https://faculty.biu.ac.il/~barilm/articles/publications/publications0024.html. Accessed December 8, 2015.

Barnett, R. D. "The Siege of Lachish." Pages 139–45 in Harry M. Orlinsky, editor. *The Israel Exploration Journal Reader.* New York: KTAV, 1981.

Bar-Oz, Guy, Ram Bouchnik, Ehud Weiss, Lior Weissbrod, Daniella E. Bar-Yosef Mayer, and Ronny Reich. "'Holy Garbage': A Quantitative Study of the City-Dump of Early Roman Jerusalem." *Levant* 39 (2007): 1–12.

Barrett, C. K. *The New Testament Background.* San Francisco: HarperSanFrancisco, 1987.

Bartlett, John R. "The Archaeology of Qumran." Pages 67–94 in John R. Bartlett, editor. *Archaeology and Biblical Interpretation.* London: Routledge, 1997.

Beck, Pirhiya. "The Drawings and Decorative Designs." Pages 143–203 in Ze'ev Meshel, editor. *Kuntillet 'Ajrud (Ḥorvat Teman): An Iron Age II Religious site on the Judah-Sinai Border.* Jerusalem: Israel Exploration Society, 2012.

Bendor, S. *The Social Structure of Ancient Israel: The Institution of the Family (Beit 'Ab) from the Settlement to the End of the Monarchy.* Jerusalem: Simor, 1996.

Berlinerblau, J. "The 'Popular Religion' Paradigm in Old Testament Research: A Sociological Critique." Pages 53–76 in David J. Chalcraft, editor. *Social-Scientific Old Testament Criticism.* Sheffield: Sheffield Academic Press, 1997.

Bernard of Morlaix. "De Contemptu Mundi." Translated by J. M. Neale. *Hymns of the Christian Church.* The Harvard Classics. 1909–14. Online: http://www.bartleby.com/45/2/114.html. Accessed July 6, 2016.

Bietak, Manfred, "Exodus Evidence: An Egyptologist Looks at Biblical History." *BAR* 42, no. 3 (1016): 31–37.

Blanton, Thomas R., IV. "Archaeology and the Historical Imagination: The Corinthians Eucharist in Architectural Context(s)." In James Riley Strange and Tom McCollough, editors. *Archaeology and the New Testament World: New Discoveries and New Frontiers.* Atlanta: Society of Biblical Literature, Forthcoming.

Blasi, Anthony J., Jean Duhaime, and Paul-André Turcotte, Editors. *Handbook of Early Christianity: Social Science Approaches.* New York: Alta Mira, 2002.

Bond, Helen K. "What Can We Know About the Roman Centurion?" *Bible Odyssey.* Online: http://www.bibleodyssey.org/en/places/related-articles/roman-centurion.aspx. Accessed September 13, 2016.

Borowski, Oded. *Daily Life in Biblical Times.* Atlanta: Society of Biblical Literature, 2003.

_____. "Eat, Drink and Be Merry: The Mediterranean Diet." *NEA* 67, no. 2 (2004): 96–107.

_____. *Every Living Thing: Daily Use of Animals in Ancient Israel.* Walnut Creek, CA: Alta Mira, 1998.

Bovon, François. *Luke 1.* Minneapolis: Fortress Press, 2002.

Braemer, Frank. *L'Architecture Domestique du Levant à l'Age du Fer.* Paris: Éditions Recherche sur les civilisations, 1982.

Brody, Aaron J. "The Archaeology of the Extended Family: A Household Compound from Iron II Tell En-Nasbeh." Pages 237–54 in Assaf Yasur-Landau, Jennie R. Ebeling, and Laura B. Mazow, editors. *Household Archaeology in Ancient Israel and Beyond.* Leiden: Brill, 2011.

Broshi, Magen, and Hanan Eshel. "Whose Bones?" *BAR* 29, no. 1 (2003): 26–33, 71.

Brothwell, Don R. *Digging Up Bones: The Excavation, Treatment and Study of Human Skeletal Remains.* London: British Museum, 1972.

Brown, Raymond E. *The Gospel According to John.* New York: Doubleday, 1966.

Bultmann, Rudolph. *History of the Synoptic Tradition.* Oxford: Basil Blackwell, 1963.

Bunimovitz, Shlomo, and Avraham Faust. "Ideology in Stone: Understanding the Four Room House." *BAR* 28, no. 4 (2002): 32–41, 59–60.

———. "Reconstructing Biblical Archaeology: Toward an Integration of Archaeology and the Bible." Pages 43–54 in Thomas E. Levy, editor. *Historical Biblical Archaeology and the Future: The New Pragmatism.* London: Routledge, 2010.

Burn, A. R. "Hic Breve Vivitur: A Study of the Expectation of Life in the Roman Empire." *Past and Present* 4 (1953): 2–31.

Cahill, Jane, et al. "It Had to Happen—Scientists Examine Remains of Ancient Bathrooms." *BAR* 17 (1991): 64–69.

Callaway, Joseph A. "A Visit with Ahilud: A Revealing Look at Village Life When Israel First Settled the Promised Land." *BAR* 9, no. 5 (1983): 42–53.

Canaan, T. *The Palestinian Arab House: Its Architecture and Folklore.* Jerusalem: Syrian Orphanage, 1933.

Carter, Charles E. "Ethnoarchaeology." *OEANE* 2.280–84.

Charlesworth, James H. "Archaeology, Jesus and Christian Faith?" Pages 1–22 in James H. Charlesworth and W. P. Weaver, editors. *What Has Archaeology to Do with Faith?* Philadelphia: Trinity, 1992.

———. "Jesus Research and Archaeology: A New Perspective." Pages 11–63 in James H. Charlesworth, editor. *Jesus and Archaeology.* Grand Rapids: Eerdmans, 2006.

Clancy, Frank. "Shishak/Shoshenq's Travels." *JSOT* 86 (1999): 3–23.

Clark, Douglas R. "Bricks, Sweat and Tears: The Human Investment in Constructing a 'Four-Room' House." *NEA* 66 (2003): 34–43.

Coale, Ansley, and Paul Demeny. *Regional Model Life Tables and Stable Populations.* New York: Academic, 1983.

Corbo, Virgilio C. "Capernaum." *ABD* I.866–69.

Crossan, John Dominic. *The Birth of Christianity: Discovering What Happened in the Years Immediately After the Execution of Jesus.* San Francisco: Harper, 1998.

———. "The Relationship between Galilean Archaeology and Historical Jesus Research." Pages 151–62 in Douglas R. Edwards and C. Thomas McCollough, editors. *The Archaeology of Difference: Gender, Ethnicity, Class and the "Other" in Antiquity, Studies in Honor of Eric M. Meyers.* Boston: American Schools of Oriental Research, 2007.

Crossan, John Dominic, and Jonathan L. Reed. *Excavating Jesus: Beneath the Stones, Behind the Texts.* San Francisco: Harper, 2001.

_____. *In Search of Paul.* San Francisco: Harper, 2004.

Currid, John D., and Avi Navon. "Iron Age Pits and the Lahav (Tell Halif) Grain Storage Project." *BASOR* 273 (1989): 67–78.

Dahood, Mitchel. *Psalms I:1–50.* Garden City, NY: Doubleday, 1966.

Dalman, Gustaf. *Arbeit und Sitte in Palästina: Band VII, Das Haus, Hühnerzucht, Taubenzucht, Bienenzucht.* Gütersloh: Bertelsmann, 1942.

Daszkiewicz, Malgorzata, Bern Liesen, and Gerwulf Schneider. "Provenance Study of Hellenistic, Roman and Byzantine Kitchen Wares from the Theatre-Temple Area of Umm Qais/Gadara, Jordan." Pages 147–58 in Bettina Fischer-Genz, Yvonne Gerber, and Hanna Hamel, editors. *Roman Pottery in the Near East: Local Production and Regional Trade.* Oxford: Archaeopress, 2014.

Davis, Thomas W. "Faith and Archaeology: A Brief History to the Present." *BAR* 19, no. 2 (1993): 54–59.

Day, John. "Asherah." *ABD* 1.483–87.

Dee, Michael W., Christopher Bronk Ramsey, and Thomas F. G. Higham. "Radiocarbon Dating and the Exodus Tradition." Pages 81–90 in Thomas E. Levy, Thomas Schneider, and William H. C. Propp, editors. *Israel's Exodus in Transdisciplinary Perspective.* New York: Springer, 2015.

Dell'Amore, Christine. "Ancient Roman Giant Found—Oldest Complete Skeleton with Gigantism." *National Geographic* (2012). Online: http://news.nationalgeographic.com/news/2012/11/121102-gigantism-ancient-skeleton-archaeology-history-science-rome/. Accessed October 5, 2015.

Demand, Nancy. *Birth, Death, and Motherhood in Classical Greece.* Baltimore: Johns Hopkins University Press, 1994.

Dessel, J. P. "In Search of a Good Book: A Critical Survey of Handbooks on Biblical Archaeology." Pages 67–98 in Milton C. Moreland, editor. *Between Text and Artifact: Integrating Archaeology in Biblical Studies Teaching.* Atlanta: Society of Biblical Literature, 2003.

Dever, William G. "Archaeology and the 'Age of Solomon': A Case Study in Archaeology and Historiography." Pages 217–51 in Lowell K. Handy, editor. *The Age of Solomon: Scholarship at the Turn of the Millennium.* Leiden: Brill, 1997.

_____. "Archaeology, History and the Bible." Pages 44–52 in P. J. Achtemeier, editor. *Harper's Bible Dictionary.* San Francisco: Harper & Row, 1985.

_____. "Asherah, Consort of Yahweh? New Evidence from Kuntillet 'Ajrûd." *BASOR* 255 (1984): 21–37.

_____. "Biblical Archaeology." *OEANE* 1.315–19.

_____. *Did God Have a Wife? Archaeology and Folk Religion in Ancient Israel.* Grand Rapids: Eerdmans, 2005.

_____. *The Lives of Ordinary People in Ancient Israel: Where Archaeology and the Bible Intersect.* Grand Rapids: Eerdmans, 2012.

_____. *Recent Archaeological Discoveries and Biblical Research.* Seattle: University of Washington Press, 1990.

_____. *What Did the Biblical Writers Know and When Did They Know It? What Archaeology Can Tell Us About the Reality of Ancient Israel.* Grand Rapids: Eerdmans, 2001.

Durand, John D. "Mortality Estimates from Roman Tombstone Inscriptions." *American Journal of Sociology* 65, no. 4 (1960): 365–73.

Eakins, J. Kenneth. "Human Osteology and Archeology." *BA* 43, no. 2 (1980): 89–96.

Ebeling, Jennie R. *Women's Lives in Biblical Times.* New York: T & T Clark, 2010.

_____. "Engendering the Israelite Harvests." *NEA* 79, no. 3 (2016): 186–94.

Edwards, James R. "Archaeology Gives New Reality to Paul's Ephesus Riot." *BAR* 42, no. 4 (2016): 24–32, 62.

Elliott, John H. *What Is Social-Scientific Criticism?* Minneapolis: Fortress Press, 1993.

Erdemgil, S., et al. *Ephesus.* Istanbul: Cemberlitas, 2000.

Éry, K. K. "Investigations on the Demographic Source Value of Tombstones Originating from the Roman Period." *Alba Regia* 10 (1969): 51–67.

Evans, Craig A. "Excavating Caiaphas, Pilate, and Simon of Cyrene: Assessing the Literary and Archaeological Evidence." Pages 323–40 in James H. Charlesworth, editor. *Jesus and Archaeology.* Grand Rapids: Eerdmans, 2006.

Facchini, F., E. Rastelli, and P. Brasili. "Cribra Orbitalia and Cribra Cranii in Roman Skeletal Remains from the Ravenna Area and Rimini (I–IV century AD)." *IJO* 14, no. 2 (2004): 126–36.

Falconer, Steven E. "Village Economy and Society in the Jordan Valley: A Study of Bronze Age Rural Complexity." Pages 121–42 in Glenn M. Schwartz and Steven E. Falconer, editors. *Archaeological Views from the Countryside: Village Communities in Early Complex Societies.* Washington, DC: Smithsonian Institution, 1994.

Faust, Avraham. *The Archaeology of Israelite Society in Iron Age II.* Winona Lake, IN: Eisenbrauns, 2012.

_____. "The Rural Community in Ancient Israel during Iron Age II." *BASOR* 317 (2000): 17–39.

Faust, Avraham, and Shlomo Bunimovitz. "The Four Room House: Embodying Iron Age Israelite Society." *NEA* 66, no. 1–2 (2003): 22–31

Fiensy, David A. *Christian Origins and the Ancient Economy.* Eugene, OR: Cascade, 2014.

_____, and James Riley Strange. *Galilee in the Late Second Temple and Mishnaic Periods Volume 1: Life, Culture, and Society*. Minneapolis: Fortress Press, 2014.

_____, and James Riley Strange. *Galilee in the Late Second Temple and Mishnaic Periods Volume 2: The Archaeological Record from Cities, Towns, and Villages*. Minneapolis: Fortress Press, 2015.

_____. *Jesus the Galilean: Soundings in a First Century Life*. Piscataway, NJ: Gorgias, 2007.

_____. "The Roman Empire and Asia Minor." Pages 36–56 in Scot McKnight and Grant R. Osborne, editors. *The Face of New Testament Studies*. Grand Rapids: Baker, 2004.

_____. *The Social History of Palestine in the Herodian Period: The Land Is Mine*. Lewiston, NY: Edwin Mellen, 1991.

_____. "Village Life." Pages 177–207 in David A. Fiensy and James Riley Strange. *Galilee in the Late Second Temple and Mishnaic Periods Volume 1: Life, Culture, and Society*. Minneapolis: Fortress Press, 2014.

Finkelstein, Israel, et al. *'Izbet Ṣarṭah: An Early Iron Age Site near Rosh Ha'ayin, Israel*. Oxford: BAR, 1986.

Finkelstein, Israel, and Neil Asher Silberman. *The Bible Unearthed: Archaeology's New Vision of Ancient Israel and the Origin of Its Sacred Texts*. New York: Touchstone, 2001.

Firmage, Edwin. "Zoology (Fauna)." *ABD* VI.1109–67.

Flusser, David. *Judaism and the Origins of Christianity*. Jerusalem: Magness, 2009 [1988].

Freyne, Seán. *Galilee from Alexander the Great to Hadrian 323 BCE to 135 CE*. Edinburgh: T & T Clark, 1980.

Frier, Bruce. "Roman Life Expectancy: The Pannonian Evidence." *Phoenix* 37, no. 4 (1983): 328–44.

_____. "Roman Life Expectancy: Ulpian's Evidence." *Harvard Studies in Classical Philology* 86 (1982): 213–51.

Fuchs, Ron. "The Palestinian Arab House and the Islamic 'Primitive Hut.'" *Muqarnas* 15 (1998): 157–77.

Fuller, Anne H. *Buarij: Portrait of a Lebanese Muslim Village*. Cambridge, MA: Harvard University Press, 1963.

Gallant, Thomas W. *Risk and Survival in Ancient Greece*. Stanford: Stanford University Press, 1991.

Gannon, Megan, Editor. "Pharaoh-Branded Amulet Found at Ancient Copper Mine in Jordan." *Live Science*. September 19, 2014. Online: 1. http://www.livescience.com/47884-pharaoh-amulet-ancient-copper-mine.html. Accessed March 28, 2016.

Garroway, Kristine. *Children in the Ancient Near Eastern Household.* Winona Lake, IN: Eisenbrauns, 2014.

Gasque, W. W. "The Historical Value of the Book of Acts." *TZ* 28 (1972): 177–96.

Geraty, Lawrence T. "Exodus Dates and Theories." Pages 55–64 in Thomas E. Levy, Thomas Schneider, and William H. C. Propp, editors. *Israel's Exodus in Transdisciplinary Perspective.* New York: Springer, 2015.

Gertoux, Gerard. "Dating Shoshenq's Campaign in Palestine." Online: https://www.academia.edu/2414472/Dating_the_Shoshenq_Is_campaign _in_Palestine. Accessed July 7, 2016.

Gibson, Shimon. *The Cave of John the Baptist: The First Archaeological Evidence of the Historical Reality of the Gospel Story.* New York: Image, 2004.

_____. *The Final Days of Jesus: The Archaeological Evidence.* New York: Harper-Collins, 2009.

Goldstein, M. S., B. Arensburg, and H. Nathan. "Skeletal Remains of Jews from the Hellenistic and Roman Periods in Israel: II. Non-metric Morphological Observations." *Bulletins et mémoires de la Société d'anthropologie de Paris* 13, no. 8 (1981): 279–95.

Gottwald, Norman. *The Tribes of Yahweh.* Maryknoll, NY: Orbis, 1979.

Govier, Gordon. "Biblical Archaeology's Top Ten Discoveries of 2013." *Christianity Today,* December 2013. Online: http://www.christianitytoday.com/ct/2013/december-web-only/biblical-archaeologys-top-ten-discoveries-of-2013.html. Accessed October 3, 2016.

Grmek, Mirko D. *Diseases in the Ancient Greek World.* Baltimore: Johns Hopkins University Press, 1989.

Groh, Dennis. "The American Field School and the Future of Biblical Archaeology." Pages 128–60 in Daniel A. Warner and Donald D. Binder, editors. *A City Set on a Hill: Essays in Honor of James F. Strange.* Mountain Home, AR: BorderStone, 2914.

Haas, N. "Anthropological Observations on the Skeletal Remains from Giv'at ha-Mivtar." *IEJ* 20 (1970): 38–60

Haas, N, and H. Nathan. "Anthropological Survey of Human Skeletal Remains from Qumran." *RevQ* 6, no. 3 (1968): 345–52.

Hachlili, Rachel. "The Goliath Family in Jericho: Funerary Inscriptions from a First Century A.D. Jewish Monumental Tomb." *BASOR* 235 (1979): 31–65.

Hachlili, Rachel, and Patricia Smith. "The Genealogy of the Goliath Family." *BASOR* 235 (1979): 67–70.

Hadas, Gideon. "Abstract: Nine Tombs of the Second Temple Period at 'En-Gedi.'" *Atiqot* 24 (1994): 1–8.

Hamilton, Victor P. "Marriage, Old Testament and Ancient Near East." *ABD* 4.559–69.

Hardin, James W. *Lahav II: Households and the Use of Domestic Space at Iron II Tell Halif: An Archaeology of Destruction.* Winona Lake, IN: Eisenbrauns, 2010.

_____. "Understanding Houses, Households, and the Levantine Archaeological Record." Pages 9–25 in Assaf Yasur-Landau, Jennie R. Ebeling, and Laura B. Mazow, editors. *Household Archaeology in Ancient Israel and Beyond.* Leiden: Brill, 2011.

Harris, Mark. "The Thera Theories: Science and the Modern Reception History of the Exodus." Pages 91–100 in Thomas E. Levy, Thomas Schneider, and William H. C. Propp, editors. *Israel's Exodus in Transdisciplinary Perspective.* New York: Springer, 2015.

Harter, S., F. Bouchet, K. Y. Mumcuoglu, and J. Zias. "Toilet Practices Among Members of the Dead Sea Scroll Sect at Qumran." *RevQ* 21 (2004): 579–84.

Hawkins, Ralph K. *How Israel Became a People.* Nashville: Abingdon, 2013.

Hayami, Akira, and Nobuko Uchida. "Size of Household in a Japanese County Throughout the Tokugawa Era." Pages 473–516 in Peter Laslett and Richard Wall, editors. *Household and Family in Past Time.* Cambridge: Cambridge University Press, 1972.

Hemer, C. J. *The Book of Acts in the Setting of Hellenistic History.* Tübingen: Mohr, 1989.

Herr, Larry G., and Gary L. Christopherson. *Excavation Manual: Madaba Plains Project.* Berrien Springs, MI: Andrews University Press, 1998.

Herz, Johannes. "Grossgrundbesitz in Palästina im Zeitalter Jesu." *PJ* 24 (1928): 98–113.

Hezser, Catherine, Editor. *The Oxford Handbook of Jewish Daily Life in Roman Palestine.* Oxford: Oxford University, 2010.

Higginbotham, Carolyn. "Shishak." *New IDB* 5.241–42.

Hirschfeld, Yizhar. "The Early Roman Bath and Fortress at Ramat Hanadiv Near Caesarea." *The Roman and Byzantine Near East: Some Recent Archaeological Research. JRA* 14 (1995): 28–55.

_____. *The Palestinian Dwelling in the Roman-Byzantine Period.* Jerusalem: Franciscan, 1995.

_____. *Ramat Hanadiv Excavations.* Jerusalem: Israel Exploration Society, 2000.

Hirschfeld, Yizhar, and Miriam Feinberg-Vamosh. "A Country Gentleman's Estate: Unearthing the Splendors of Ramat Hanadiv." *BAR* 31, no. 2 (2005): 18–31.

Hoffmeier, James K. *Israel in Egypt: The Evidence for the Authenticity of the Exodus Tradition.* New York: Oxford University Press, 1996.

_____. "Out of Egypt: The Archaeological Context of the Exodus." Pages 1–20 in Margaret Warker, editor. *Ancient Israel in Egypt and the Exodus.* Washington, DC: Biblical Archaeological Society, 2012. Online: https://www.academia.edu/22074175/Ancient_Israel_in_Egypt_and_the_Exodus?auto=view& campaign=weekly_digest. Accessed March 29, 2016.

Holladay Jr., John S. "House, Israelite." *ABD* III.308–18.

Holladay, William L. *A Concise Hebrew and Aramaic Lexicon of the Old Testament.* Grand Rapids: Eerdmans, 1988.

Homsher, Robert S. "Mud Bricks and the Process of Construction in the Middle Bronze Age Southern Levant." *BASOR* 368 (2012): 1–27.

Hopkins, David. *The Highlands of Canaan.* Sheffield: Almond, 1985.

Hopkins, Keith. "On the Probable Age Structure of the Roman Population." *Population Studies.* 20 (1966): 245–64.

Hoppe, Leslie J. *What Are They Saying About Biblical Archaeology?* New York: Paulist, 1984.

Horsley, G. H. R. "The Inscriptions of Ephesus and the New Testament." *NovT* 34 (1992): 105–68.

Huebner, Sabine R. "A Mediterranean Family? A Comparative Approach to the Ancient World." Pages 3–26 in Sabine R. Huebner and Geoffrey Nathan, editors. *Mediterranean Families in Antiquity: Households, Extended Families, and Domestic Space.* Oxford: Wiley-Blackwell, 2016. Online at: https://www.academia.edu/26034682/_A_Mediterranean_Family_A_Comparative_Approach _to_the_Ancient_World_in_Sabine_R._Huebner_and_Geoffrey_Nathan_ed s._Mediterranean_Families_in_Antiquity_Households_Extended_Families _and_Domestic_Space._Oxford_Wiley-Blackwell_2016_3-26. Accessed July 12, 2016.

Ilan, Tal. *Integrating Women into Second Temple Judaism.* Peabody, MA: Hendrickson, 1999.

Jensen, Morton Hørning. "Rural Galilee and Rapid Changes: An Investigation of the Socio-Economic Dynamics and Developments in Roman Galilee." *Bib* 93 (2012): 43–67.

Kee, Howard Clark. *Christian Origins in Sociological Perspective: Methods and Resources.* Philadelphia: Westminster, 1980.

Keenleyside, A., and K. Panayotova. "Cribra Orbitalia and Porotic Hyperostosis in a Greek Colonial Population (5th to 3rd centuries BC) from the Black Sea." *IJO* 16, no. 5 (2006): 373–84.

Kenyon, Kathleen. *Beginning in Archaeology.* New York: Praeger, 1961.

Killebrew, Ann E. "Between Heaven and Earth: Educational Perspectives on the Archaeology and Material Culture of the Bible." Pages 11–30 in Milton C. Moreland, editor. *Between Text and Artifact: Integrating Archaeology in Biblical Studies Teaching.* Atlanta: Society of Biblical Literature, 2003.

King, J. Philip, and Lawrence E. Stager. *Life in Biblical Israel.* Louisville: Westminster John Knox, 2001.

Kitchen, K. A. *On the Reliability of the Old Testament.* Grand Rapids: Eerdmans, 2003.

_____. "Shishak's Military Campaign in Israel Confirmed." *BAR* 15, no. 3 (1989): 32–33.

Klassen, William. "Judas and Jesus: A Message on a Drinking Vessel of the Second Temple Period." Pages 503–20 in James H. Charlesworth, editor. *Jesus and Archaeology.* Grand Rapids: Eerdmans, 2006.

Koester, Helmut. "Ephesus in Early Christian Literature." Pages 119–40 in H. Koester, editor. *Ephesos, Metropolis of Asia: An Interdisciplinary Approach to Its Archaeology, Religion, and Culture.* Valley Forge, PA: Trinity, 1995.

Kramer, Carol. *Village Ethnoarchaeology: Rural Iran in Archaeological Perspective.* New York: Academic, 1982.

Krijgsman, Marten. "Biblical Studies in the Light of Archaeological Theory." Online: https://www.academia.edu/28430164/Biblical_Studies_in_the_Light_of_Archaeological_Theory?auto=download&campaign=weekly_digest. Accessed October 3, 2016.

LaBianca, Øystein S. "Everyday Life at Hesban Through the Centuries." Pages 197–209 in David Merling and Lawrence T. Geraty, editors. *Hesban After 25 Years.* Berrien Springs, MI: Andrews University Press, 1994.

Lance, H. Darrell. *The Old Testament and the Archaeologist.* Philadelphia: Fortress Press, 1981.

Lang, Bernhard, Editor. *Anthropological Approaches to the Old Testament.* Philadelphia: Fortress Press, 1985.

Laslett, Peter. "Mean Household Size in England Since the Sixteenth Century." Pages 125–58 in Peter Laslett and Richard Wall, editors. *Household and Family in Past Time.* Cambridge: Cambridge University Press, 1972.

Laughlin, John C. H. "Capernaum from Jesus' Time and After." *BAR* 19, no. 5 (1993): 54–61, 90.

_____. "On the Convergence of Texts and Artifacts: Using Archaeology to Teach the Hebrew Bible." Pages 115–32 in Milton C. Moreland, editor. *Between Text and Artifact: Integrating Archaeology in Biblical Studies Teaching.* Atlanta: Society of Biblical Literature, 2003.

Levine, Lee I. "Archaeological Discoveries from the Greco-Roman Era." Pages 75–88 in Hershel Shanks and Benjamin Mazar, editors. *Recent Archaeology in the Land of Israel.* Washington, DC: Biblical Archaeology Society, 1984.

_____. "The Synagogues of Galilee." Pages 129–50 in David A. Fiensy and James Riley Strange, editors. *Galilee in the Late Second Temple and Mishnaic Periods Volume 1: Life, Culture, and Society.* Minneapolis: Fortress Press, 2014.

Levy, Thomas E. "The New Pragmatism: Integrating Anthropological, Digital, and Historical Biblical Archaeologies." Pages 3–42 in Thomas E. Levy, editor.

Historical Biblical Archaeology and the Future: The New Pragmatism. London: Routledge, 2010.

Levy, Thomas E., Thomas Schneider, and William H. C. Propp, Editors. *Israel's Exodus in Transdisciplinary Perspective: Text, Archaeology, Culture, and Geoscience.* New York: Springer, 2015.

Levy, Thomas E., Stefan Münger, and Mohammad Najjar. "A Newly Discovered Scarab of Sheshonq I: Recent Iron Age Explorations in Southern Jordan." *Antiquity Journal: A Review of World Archaeology.* Online: http://journal.antiquity.ac.uk/projgall/levy341. Accessed March 28, 2016.

London, Gloria. "Ethnoarchaeology and Interpretations of the Past." *NEA* 63, no. 1 (2000): 2–8.

De Luca, Stefano, and Anna Lena. "Magdala, Taricheae." Pages 280–342 in David A. Fiensy and James Riley Strange, editors. *Galilee in the Late Second Temple and Mishnaic Periods Volume 2: The Archaeological Record from Cities, Towns, and Villages.* Minneapolis: Fortress Press, 2015.

Lutfiyya, Abdulla M. *Baytin: A Jordanian Village.* London: Mouton, 1966.

MacDonald, Nathan. *What Did the Ancient Israelites Eat?* Grand Rapids: Eerdmans, 2008.

Mack, Burton. *A Myth of Innocence.* Philadelphia: Fortress Press, 1988.

Magen, Y. *The Stone Vessel Industry in the Second Temple Period.* Jerusalem: Israel Exploration Society, 2002.

Magness, Jodi. *Stone and Dung, Oil and Spit: Jewish Daily Life in the Time of Jesus.* Grand Rapids: Eerdmans, 2011.

Malina, Bruce. *The New Testament World: Insights from Cultural Anthropology.* Atlanta: John Knox, 1981.

Marshall, I. Howard. *Commentary on Luke.* Grand Rapids: Eerdmans, 1978.

Mattilah, Sharon Lea. "Capernaum, Village of Nahum, from Hellenistic to Byzantine Times." Pages 217–57 in David A. Fiensy and James Riley Strange, editors. *Galilee in the Late Second Temple and Mishnaic Periods Volume 2: The Archaeological Record from Cities, Towns, and Villages.* Minneapolis: Fortress Press, 2015.

Mazar, Amihai. "The 1997-1998 Excavations at Tel Rehov: Preliminary Report." *IEJ* 49 (1999): 1–42.

_____. *Archaeology of the Land of the Bible: 10,000-586 B.C.E.* New York: Doubleday, 1990.

McRay, John. *Archaeology and the New Testament.* Grand Rapids: Baker, 1991.

Meshel, Ze'ev. "The Nature of the Site and Its Background." Pages 65–69 in Ze'ev Meshel, editor. *Kuntillet 'Ajrud (Ḥorvat Teman): An Iron Age II Religious Site on the Judah-Sinai Border.* Jerusalem: Israel Exploration Society, 2012.

Meyers, Carol. "Archaeology—A Window to the Lives of Israelite Women."

Pages 61–108 in Irmtraud Fischer, Mercedes Navarro Puerto, and Adriana Taschl-Erber, editors. *Torah*. Atlanta: Society of Biblical Literature, 2011.

_____. "The Family in Early Israel." Pages 1–47 in Leo G. Perdue, Joseph Blenkinsopp, John J. Collins, and Carol Meyers, editors. *Families in Ancient Israel*. Louisville: Westminster John Knox, 1997.

_____. "From Field Crops to Food: Attributing Gender and Meaning to Bread Production in Iron Age Israel." Pages 67–84 in Douglas R. Edwards and C. Thomas McCollough, editors. *The Archaeology of Difference: Gender, Ethnicity, Class and the 'Other' in Antiquity*. Boston: American Schools of Oriental Research, 2007.

_____. "Material Remains and Social Relations: Women's Culture in Agrarian Households of the Iron Age." Pages 425–44 in William G. Dever and Seymour Gitin, editors. *Symbiosis, Symbolism, and the Power of the Past: Canaan, Ancient Israel, and Their Neighbors from the Late Bronze Age through Roman Palaestina*. Winona Lake, IN: Eisenbrauns, 2003.

_____. *Rediscovering Eve: Ancient Israelite Women in Context*. Oxford: Oxford University Press, 2013.

_____. "Was Ancient Israel a Patriarchal Society?" *JBL* 133, no. 1 (2014): 8–27.

Meyers, Eric M. "The Bible and Archaeology." *BA* 47 (1984): 36–40.

_____. "The Bible and Archaeology." Pages lvii–lxi in Harold Attridge, editor. *The HarperCollins Study Bible*. New York: HarperCollins, 2006.

_____. "New Testament and Archaeology: When and How They Developed as a Distinct Field." In James Riley Strange and Tom McCollough, editors. *Archaeology and the New Testament World: New Discoveries and New Frontiers*. Atlanta: Society of Biblical Literature, Forthcoming.

_____. "The Use of Archaeology in Understanding Rabbinic Materials: An Archaeological Perspective." Pages 303–19 in Steven Fine and Aaron Koller, editors. *Talmuda De-eretz Israel: Archaeology and the Rabbis in Late Antique Palestine*. Boston: De Gruyter, 2014.

Meyers, Eric M., and James F. Strange. *Archaeology, the Rabbis and Early Christianity*. Nashville: Abingdon, 1981.

Meyers, Eric M., and Carol Meyers. "Holy Land Archaeology: Where the Past Meets the Present." *Buried History* 50 (2014): 3–16.

Minozzi, S., W. Pantano, P. Catalano, F. di Gennaro, and G. Fornaciari. "The Roman Giant: Overgrowth Syndrome in Skeletal Remains from the Imperial Age." *IJO* 25, no. 4 (2015): 574–84.

Mitchell, Piers D. "Child's Health in the Crusader Period Inhabitants of Tel Jezreel, Israel." *Levant* 38 (2006): 37–44.

_____. "The Palaeopathology of Skulls Recovered from a Medieval Cave Cemetery near Safed, Israel (Thirteenth to Seventeenth Century)." *Levant* 36 (2004): 243–50.

Mitchell, Piers D., and Y. Tepper. "Intestinal Parasitic Worm Eggs from a Crusader Period Cesspool in the City of Acre (Israel)." *Levant* 39 (2007): 91–95.

Moreland, Milton C. "Archaeology in New Testament Courses." Pages 133–49 in Milton C. Moreland, editor. *Between Text and Artifact: Integrating Archaeology in Biblical Studies Teaching.* Atlanta: Society of Biblical Literature, 2003.

Moreland, Milton C., Shannon Burkes, and Melissa Aubin. "Introduction: Between Text and Artifact." Pages 1–10 in Milton C. Moreland, editor. *Between Text and Artifact: Integrating Archaeology in Biblical Studies Teaching.* Atlanta: Society of Biblical Literature, 2003.

Moorsom, Robert Maude. *A Historical Companion to Hymns Ancient and Modern.* London: Clay & Sons, 1903.

Morris, Ian. "Archaeology, Standards of Living and Greek Economic History." Pages 91–126 in J. G. Manning and Ian Morris, editors. *The Ancient Economy.* Stanford: Stanford University Press, 2005.

Moyer, James C., and Victor H. Matthews. "The Use and Abuse of Archaeology in Current Bible Handbooks." *BA* 48, no. 3 (1985): 149–59.

Mullins, Robert A. "The Emergence of Israel in Retrospect." Pages 517–26 in Thomas E. Levy, Thomas Schneider, and William H. C. Propp, editors. *Israel's Exodus in Transdisciplinary Perspective.* New York: Springer, 2015.

Mussies, G. "Pagans, Jews, and Christians at Ephesus." Pages 177–94 in G. Mussies and P. W. van der Horst, editors. *Studies on the Hellenistic Background of the New Testament.* Utrecht: Faculteit der Godgeleerheid van der Rijksuniversiteit, 1990.

Nagar, Yossi, and Flavia Sonntag. "Byzantine Period Burials in the Negev: Anthropological Description and Summary." *IEJ* 58 (2008): 79–93.

Nagar, Yossi, and Hagit Torgeé. "Biological Characteristics of Jewish Burials in the Hellenistic and Early Roman Periods." *IEJ* 53 (2003): 164–71.

Nakhai, Beth Alpert. "Embracing the Domestic." Page 37 in *40 Futures: Experts Predict What's Next for Biblical Archaeology.* Washington, DC: Biblical Archaeology Society, 2015.

Nathan, H. "Skeletal Remains from Naḥal Ḥever." *Atiqot* 3 (1961): 165–75.

Netzer, Ehud. "Domestic Architecture in the Iron Age." Pages 193–201 in Aharon Kempinski and Ronny Reich, editors. *The Architecture of Ancient Israel.* Jerusalem: Israel Exploration Society, 1992.

Neufeld, Dietmar, and Richard E. Demaris, editors. *Understanding the Social World of the New Testament.* London: Routledge, 2010.

Neufeld, Edward. "Hygiene Conditions in Ancient Israel (Iron Age)." Pages

151–79 in E. F. Campbell Jr. and D. N. Freedman, editors. *The Biblical Archaeologist Reader IV.* Sheffield: Almond, 1983.

Neusner, Jacob. "Archaeology and Babylonian Jewry." Pages 331–43 in James A. Sanders, editor. *Near Eastern Archaeology in the Twentieth Century.* Garden City, NY: Doubleday, 1970.

Neyrey, J. H., and E. C. Stewart, Editors. *The Social World of the New Testament.* Peabody, MA: Hendrickson, 2008.

Nigro, Lorenzo. "Tell es-Sultan: A Pilot Project for Archaeology in Palestine." *NEA* 79, no. 1 (2016): 4–17.

No author. "Bubastite Portal," *Wikipedia.* Online: https://en.wikipedia.org/wiki/Bubastite_Portal. Accessed March 14, 2016.

No author. "The Bubastite Portal: Reliefs and Inscriptions at Karnack," Volume III, The University of Chicago Oriental Institute Publications, Volume LXXIV. Online: http://oi.uchicago.edu/sites/oi.uchicago.edu/files/uploads/shared/docs/oip74.pdf. Accessed March 15, 2016.

No author. "The Excavation Process: How We Excavate." Online: https://www.youtube.com/watch?v=PcT1vGyJzyg. Accessed April 28, 2016.

No author. "Howard Carter." *Wikipedia.* Online: https://en.wikipedia.org/wiki/Howard_Carter.

No author. "Human Height." *Wikipedia.* Online: https://en.wikipedia.org/wiki/Human_height. Accessed November 16, 2015.

No author. "Introduction to Archaeology: Glossary." *Archaeological Institute of America.* Online: https://www.archaeological.org/education/glossary.

No author. "Life Expectancy at Birth." *World Fact Book.* Online: https://www.cia.gov/library/publications/the-world-factbook/rankorder/2102rank.html. Accessed November 16, 2015.

No author. "List of Countries by Life Expectancy." *Wikipedia.* Online: https://en.wikipedia.org/wiki/List_of_countries_by_life_expectancy. Accessed November 16, 2015.

No author. *Tel Gezer Excavation Manual: Unedited & Preliminary Draft May 2006.* Online: http://www.telgezer.com/gezer/assets/file/telgezer_excavation-manual.pdf. Accessed May 14, 2016.

Nolland, John. *The Gospel of Matthew.* Grand Rapids: Eerdmans, 2005.

Oakes, Peter. *Reading Romans in Pompeii: Paul's Letter at Ground Zero.* Minneapolis: Fortress Press, 2009.

Oakman, Douglas. *Jesus and the Peasants.* Eugene, OR: Cascade, 2008.

Oliver, J. H. *The Sacred Gerusia.* Baltimore: American School of Classical Studies, 1941.

Osiek, C. *What Are They Saying About the Social Setting of the New Testament?* New York: Paulist, 1992.

Oster, Richard. "A Historical Commentary on the Missionary Success Stories in Acts 19:11-40." PhD diss., Princeton University, 1974.

Parker, Henry Michael Denn. "Manipulus." Page 644 in H. G. L. Hammon and H. H. Scullard, editors. *The Oxford Classical Dictionary.* Oxford: Clarendon, 1970.

Parker, Henry Michael Denn, and George Ronald Watson. "Centurio." Page 222 in H. G. L. Hammon and H. H. Scullard, editors. *The Oxford Classical Dictionary.* Oxford: Clarendon, 1970.

_____. "Cohors." Page 258 in H. G. L. Hammon and H. H. Scullard, editors. *The Oxford Classical Dictionary.* Oxford: Clarendon, 1970.

Parkin, Tim G. *Demography and Roman Society.* Baltimore: Johns Hopkins University Press, 1992.

Piontek, J., and T. Kozlowsk. "Frequency of Cribra Orbitalia in the Subadult Medieval Population from Gruczno, Poland." *International Journal of Osteoarchaeology* 12, no. 3 (2002): 202–8.

Pritchard, James B. *The Ancient Near East in Pictures Relating to the Old Testament.* Princeton: Princeton University Press, 1954.

_____. *The Ancient Near East: Volume I An Anthology of Texts and Pictures.* Princeton: Princeton University Press, 1958.

Rainey, Anson F., and R. Steven Notley. *The Sacred Bridge: Carta's Atlas of the Biblical World.* Jerusalem: Carta, 2006.

Redford, Donald. "Shishak." *ABD* 5.1221–22.

Reed, Jonathan L. *Archaeology and the Galilean Jesus.* Harrisburg, PA: Trinity, 2000.

_____. "Instability in Jesus' Galilee: A Demographic Perspective." *JBL* 129, no. 2 (2010): 343–65.

Reinhard, Karl J., and Adauto Araújo. "Archaeoparasitology." Pages 494–501 in Deborah M. Pearsall, editor. *Encyclopedia of Archaeology.* Amsterdam: Elsevier, 2008.

Rohrbaugh, Richard L., editor. "Introduction." Pages 1–15 in Richard. L. Rohrbaugh, editor. *The Social Sciences and New Testament Interpretation.* Peabody, MA: Hendrickson, 1996.

_____. *The Social Sciences and New Testament Interpretation.* Peabody, MA: Hendrickson, 1996.

Röhrer-Ertl, Olav. "Facts and Results Based on Skeletal Remains from Qumran Found in the *Collectio Kurth*: A Study in Methodology." Pages 181–93 in Katharina Galor, Jean-Baptiste Humbert, and Jürgen Zangenberg, editors. *Qumran: The Site of the Dead Sea Scrolls. Archaeological Interpretations and Debates. Proceedings of a Conference Held at Brown University, November 17-19, 2002.* Leiden: Brill, 2006.

Rosen, Baruch. "Subsistence Economy of Stratum II." Pages 156–85 in Israel

Finkelstein et al. *'Izbet Ṣarṭah: An Early Iron Age Site near Rosh Ha'ayin, Israel.* Oxford: BAR, 1986.

Roser, Max. "Child Mortality." *OurWorldInData.org.* Online: http://ourworldin-data.org/data/population-growth-vital-statistics/child-mortality/. Accessed December 4, 2015.

Russell, J. C. *The Control of Late Ancient and Medieval Population.* Philadelphia: American Philosophical Society, 1985.

_____. *Late Ancient and Medieval Population.* Philadelphia: American Philosophical Society, 1958.

Sah, Raaj K. "The Effects of Child Mortality Changes on Fertility Choice and Parental Welfare." *Journal of Political Economy* 99, no. 3 (1991): 582–606.

Sapir-Hen, Lidar, Yuval Gadot, and Israel Finkelstein. "Animal Economy in a Temple City and Its Countryside: Iron Age Jerusalem as a Case Study." *BASOR* 375 (2016): 103–18.

Shafer-Elliott, Cynthia. *Food in Ancient Judah: Domestic Cooking in the Time of the Hebrew Bible.* Sheffield: Equinox, 2013.

Scheidel, Walter. *Death on the Nile: Disease and the Demography of Roman Egypt.* Leiden: Brill, 2001.

_____. "Population and Demography." *Princeton/Stanford Working Papers in Classics* (2006). Online: https://www.princeton.edu/~pswpc/pdfs/scheidel/040604.pdf. Accessed October 2, 2015.

_____. "Real Wages in Early Economies: Evidence for Living Standards from 1800 BCE to 1300 CE." *Princeton/Stanford Working Papers in Classics* (2009). http://www.princeton.edu/~pswpc/papers/authorMZ/scheidel/scheidel.html. Accessed March 6, 2012.

Schloen, J. David. *The House of the Father as Fact and Symbol: Patrimonialism in Ugarit and the Ancient Near East.* Winona Lake, IN: Eisenbrauns, 2001.

Schürer, Emil, Geza Vermes, and Fergus Miller. *The History of the Jewish People in the Age of Jesus Christ (175 B.C.-A.D. 135): Volume I.* Edinburgh: T & T Clark, 1973.

Schulze, Jürgen P., et al. "The WAVE and 3D: How the Waters Might Have Parted—Visualizing Evidence for a Major Volcanic Eruption in the Mediterranean and Its Impact on Exodus Models." Pages 161–72 in Thomas E. Levy, Thomas Schneider, and William H. C. Propp, editors. *Israel's Exodus in Transdisciplinary Perspective.* New York: Springer, 2015.

Seidemann, Ryan M. "Bones of Contention: A Comparative Examination of Law Governing Human Remains from Archaeological Contexts in Formerly Colonial Countries." *Louisiana Law Review* 64 (2004): 545–88.

Sheridan, Susan Guise. "Skeletal Remains from the Cemetery of Qumran: The French Collection" (2002). Online at: http://www3.nd.edu/~qumran/QumranBrown.pdf. Accessed December 10, 2015.

Sherwin-White, A. N. *Roman Society and Roman Law in the New Testament.* Oxford: Oxford University Press, 1963.

Shiloh, Yigal. "The Four-Room House: Its Situation and Function in the Israelite City." *IEJ* 20 (1970): 180–90.

_____. "The Population of Iron Age Palestine in the Light of a Sample Analysis of Urban Plans, Areas, and Population Density." *BASOR* 239 (1980): 25–35.

Siegel-Itzkovich, Judy. "Orthodox Jews Demand University Bury Its Bones." *British Medical Journal* (May 5, 2001). Online at http://www.ncbi.nlm.nih.gov/pmc/articles/PMC1773291/. Accessed December 20, 2015.

Smith, Patricia. "An Approach to the Paleodemographic Analysis of Human Skeletal Remains from Archaeological Sites." Pages 2–13 in Joseph Aviram and Allen-Paris Siddur, editors. *Biblical Archaeology Today: Proceedings of the Second International Congress on Biblical Archaeology: Pre-Congress Symposium, Population, Production and Power, Jerusalem, June 1990, Supplement, Volume 2.* Jerusalem: Israel Exploration Society, 1993.

_____. "The Human Skeletal Remains from the Abba Cave." *IEJ* 27 (1977): 121–24.

_____. "Skeletal Analysis." *OEANE,* 5.51–56.

Smith, Patricia, and Joseph Zias. "Skeletal Remains from the Late Hellenistic French Hill Tomb." *IEJ* 30 (1980): 109–15.

Smith, Patricia, Elizabeth Bornemann, and Joseph Zias. "The Skeletal Remains." Pages 110–20 in Eric M. Meyers, James F. Strange, and Carol L. Meyers, editors. *Excavations at Ancient Meiron, Upper Galilee, Israel 1971-72, 1974-75, 1977.* Cambridge, MA: ASOR, 1981.

Sofaer, Joanna R. *The Body as Material Culture: A Theoretical Osteoarchaeology.* Cambridge: Cambridge University Press, 2006.

Stager, Lawrence E. "The Archaeology of the Family in Ancient Israel." *BASOR* 260 (1985): 1–35.

Starbuck, Scott R. A. "Why Declare the Things Forbidden? Classroom Integration of Ancient Near Eastern Archaeology with Biblical Studies in Theological Context." Pages 99–113 in Milton C. Moreland, editor. *Between Text and Artifact: Integrating Archaeology in Biblical Studies Teaching.* Atlanta: Society of Biblical Literature, 2003.

Stark, Rodney. *The Rise of Christianity.* San Francisco: Harper, 1996.

Steckoll, S. H. "Marginal Notes on the Qumran Excavations." *RevQ* 7 (1969): 33–40.

_____. "Preliminary Excavation Report in the Qumran Cemetery." *RevQ* 6 (1968): 323–44.

Stegemann, Wolfgang. *The Jesus Movement: A Social History of Its First Century.* Minneapolis: Fortress Press, 1999.

Steinberg, Naomi. *The World of the Child in the Hebrew Bible.* Sheffield: Sheffield University Press, 2013.

Strack, H., and P. Billerbeck. *Kommentar zum Neuen Testament aus Talmud und Midrasch.* 4 vols. München: Beck, 1924.

Strange, James F. "The Sayings of Jesus and Archaeology." Pages 291–305 in J. H. Charlesworth and L. L. Johns, editors. *Hillel and Jesus.* Minneapolis: Fortress Press, 1997.

_____. "Tombs, the New Testament, and the Archaeology of Religion." *RevExp* 106 (2009): 399–419.

Strange, James F., D. E. Groh, and T. R. Longstaff. "Excavations at Sepphoris: The Location and Identification of Shikhin." *IEJ* 44 (1994): 216–27.

Strange, James F., Thomas R. Longstaff, Dennis E. Groh, and James Riley Strange. *The Excavations at Shikhin: Manual for Area Supervisors.* Birmingham, AL: Samford University Press, 2013.

Sweet, Louise E. *Tell Toqaan: A Syrian Village.* Ann Arbor: University of Michigan Press, 1974.

Tannous, A. I. "The Arab Village Community of the Middle East." *Annual Report of the Board of Regents of the Smithsonian Institution* (1944): 523–43.

Theissen, Gerd. *Sociology of Early Palestinian Christianity.* Philadelphia: Fortress Press, 1977.

Theissen, Gerd, and Annette Merz. *The Historical Jesus: A Comprehensive Guide.* Minneapolis: Fortress Press, 1998.

Thiel, Winfried. "Jehu." *ABD* 3.670–73.

Thompson, William M. *The Land and the Book.* 1877. Reprint, Hartford, CT: Scranton, 1910.

Trebilco, Paul. "Asia." Pages 291–362 in D. S. J. Gill and C. Gempf, editors. *The Book of Acts in Its Graeco-Roman Setting.* Grand Rapids: Eerdmans, 1994.

Tzaferis, V. "Jewish Tombs at and near Giv'at ha-Mivtar, Jerusalem." *IEJ* 20 (1970): 18–32.

Uehlinger, Christoph. "Clio in a World of Pictures—Another Look at the Lachish Reliefs from Sennacherib's Southwest Palace at Nineveh." Pages 221–305 in Lester L. Grabbe, editor. *Like a Bird in a Cage: The Invasion of Sennacherib in 701 BCE.* Sheffield: University of Sheffield Press, 2003.

Ussishkin, David. *Biblical Lachish: A Tale of Construction, Destruction, Excavation, and Restoration.* Jerusalem: Israel Exploration Society, 2014.

_____. *The Conquest of Lachish by Sennacherib.* Tel Aviv: Tel Aviv University Press, 1982.

De Vaux, R. *Archaeology and the Dead Sea Scrolls.* London: Oxford University Press, 1973.

_____. "On the Right and Wrong Uses of Archaeology." Pages 64–80 in James

A. Sanders, editor. *Near Eastern Archaeology in the Twentieth Century*. Garden City, NY: Doubleday, 1970.

Walker, P. L., R. R. Bathurst, R. Richman, T. Gjerdrum, and V. A. Andrushko. "The Causes of Porotic Hyperostosis and Cribra Orbitalia: A Reappraisal of the Iron-deficiency-anemia Hypothesis." *American Journal of Physical Anthropology* 139, no. 2 (2009): 109–25. Online: http://www.ncbi.nlm.nih.gov/pubmed/19280675.

Weiss, Ehud, and Mordechai E. Kisley. "Weeds and Seeds" *BAR* 30, no. 6 (2004): 32–37.

Wells, Calvin. "Ancient Obstetric Hazards and Female Mortality." *Bulletin of the New York Academy of Medicine* 51 (1975): 1235–41.

Wood, Bryant G. "Excavations at Kh. el-Maqatir 1995–2000, 2009–2013: A Border Fortress in the Highlands of Canaan and a Proposed New Location for the Ai of Joshua 7–8." *Associates for Biblical Research* (2014): Online: http://www.bibleinterp.com/PDFs/BibleInterp_2013_report.pdf. Accessed October 6, 2016.

Wiener, Malcolm H. "Dating the Theran Eruption: Archaeological Science Versus Nonsense Science." Pages 131–46 in Thomas E. Levy, Thomas Schneider, and William H. C. Propp, editors. *Israel's Exodus in Transdisciplinary Perspective*. New York: Springer, 2015.

Wilson, J. A. "Shishak." *IDB* 4.337–38.

Wilson, Robert R. *Sociological Approaches to the Old Testament*. Philadelphia: Fortress Press, 1984.

Wright, C. J. H. "Family." *ABD* 2.761–69.

Wright, George E. "Israelite Daily Life." *BA* 18 (1955): 50–79.

_____. "What Archaeology Can and Cannot Do." *BA* 34 (1971): 70–76.

Wright N. T. *Jesus and the Victory of God*. Minneapolis: Fortress Press, 1996.

Yamauchi, E. M. *New Testament Cities in Western Asia Minor*. Grand Rapids: Baker, 1980.

Zangenberg, Jürgen. "Archaeology and the New Testament." Pages lxii–lxvi in Harold Attridge, editor. *The HarperCollins Study Bible*. New York: HarperCollins, 2006.

Zias, Joseph. "Anthropological Analysis of Human Skeletal Remains." Pages 117–21 in Gideon Avni and Avi Greenhut, editors. *The Akeldama Tombs*. Jerusalem: Israel Antiquities Authority, 1996.

_____. "Appendix A: Anthropological Observations." *Atiqot* 19 (1990): 125.

_____. "The Cemeteries of Qumran and Celibacy: Confusion Laid to Rest?" Pages 444–71 in James H. Charlesworth, editor. *Jesus and Archaeology*. Grand Rapids: Eerdmans, 2006.

_____. "Death and Disease in Ancient Israel." *BA* 54 (1991): 147–59.

_____. "Human Skeletal Remains from a Second Temple-Period Tomb in Arnona, Jerusalem." *Atiqot: English Series* 54 (2006): 117–20.

_____. "Human Skeletal Remains from the Caiaphas Tomb." *Atiqot: English Series* 21 (1992): 78–80.

_____. "Human Skeletal Remains from the Mount Scopus Tomb." *Atiqot: English Series* 21 (1992): 97–103.

Subject Index

sociology (sociological interpretation), ix, 100, 100n5, 144, 157
stature, 75, 106–8, 107n29
stone vessels, 4
synchronism, 19

Tannaim, 114
terrace, 72, 85, 87–89
terra cotta, 41, 56
theater, 42–48
Thera (Santorini), 46, 46n81, 147, 158
top plan, 4–5
Tutankhamun, 63
Tyrannus, 39

upper story, 76. See also *'aliyyah*

village, 8–9, 15, 19, 26, 30, 48–49, 53, 58–59, 59nn126–27, 61, 63, 66n6, 67n10, 68–69, 69n16, 69n19, 70–71, 71n23, 72, 73n40, 74, 76, 76n54, 78n66, 79, 79n69, 80, 80n76, 81, 81n78, 83–84, 84n90, 85–89, 86n92, 86n95–98, 87n100, 88n109, 89n109, 89n112, 89n115, 92, 92n123, 94–95, 123, 125–26, 139, 140, 142, 144–45, 149–50, 157

widows, 120
windows, 14, 78–79, 79n69, 99

Scripture Index